Live Wires

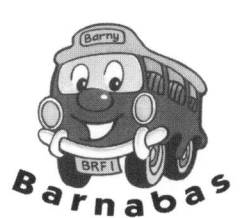

LIVE

by
Robin Sharples

Illustrated by
Simon Smith

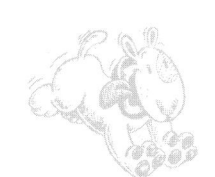

Barnabas

Text copyright © Robin Sharples 1998
Illustrations copyright © Simon Smith 1998

The author asserts the moral right to
be identified as the author of this work

Published by
The Bible Reading Fellowship
Peter's Way, Sandy Lane West
Oxford OX4 5HG
ISBN 0 7459 3562 1

First edition 1998

10 9 8 7 6 5 4 3 2 1 0

Acknowledgments
Unless otherwise stated, scripture quotations are taken
from the Good News Bible published by The Bible
Societies/HarperCollins Publishers Ltd UK
© American Bible Society, 1966, 1971, 1976, 1992.

A catalogue record for this book
is available from the British Library

Printed and bound in Malta
by Interprint Limited

CONTENTS

Christmas term

1. Creation   9
2. Brotherly love   13
3. The creation of a nation   17
4. The story of Ruth   24
5. Belonging   28
6. Parables of Jesus   32
7. Fingerprints   35
8. Jesus is coming   39
9. Elizabeth and Zechariah   43
10. Jesus is born   47

Spring term

1. God calls Moses   53
2. Teamwork   57
3. The city of peace—Jerusalem   61
4. Songs of praise to a faithful God   64
5. Jesus' childhood and baptism   67
6. Jesus in the desert   70
7. Follow me   73
8. Making an entry   77
9. Sadness and death   81
10. Celebration   85

Summer term

1. Moses and ten timely tips   91
2. Jesus teaches about lifestyle   94
3. Zacchaeus   97
4. Daniel and God's faithfulness   100
5. The Son of God   103
6. Weakness and strength   106
7. Paul's journeys (1)   109
8. Paul's journeys (2)   113
9. Commitment   116
10. Looking after God's world   120

Voucher offer   127

 # Introductory notes

The material in this book is aimed primarily at church-based or church-sponsored groups. It is designed to complement the material in the *Livewires* Bible adventures and to enhance your work with children in a way that will affirm them in their faith and their lives. Its main purpose is to act rather like a fertilizer, encouraging and nurturing growth both in relationships and in knowledge in a fresh and dynamic way.

Each session has been designed with three things in mind:

◎ **that children (and adults) spend time and effort in reading the Bible for themselves**

◎ **that the sessions relate to, but do not repeat, the material in the *Livewires* books**

◎ **that each section offers a range of elements which explore and interpret the theme**

The material is designed not just to provide a set session planner but as a resource bank to enable you to tailor your programmes to suit your need. For example, some of the sections contain activities which you may wish to stretch over several weeks.

For some of the material you might need reference books to research certain details, such as acclamations and fanfares in temple rituals. It is a good idea to encourage the children also to look things up for themselves, as well as letting them see that you have done so. Bible dictionaries, encyclopedias, atlases and concordances can all be a good way to help your group develop their research skills. To interact with them in this way will also serve to help them 'get into' the Bible and learn to access it for themselves rather than expecting others—parents, teachers and ministers, for example—to do it for them. Reading the Bible is rather like playing cricket—you *can* only learn to do it by experience; no amount of passive teaching ever quite prepares you for the shock of a fast ball or the thrill of a first catch!

Each session comprises the following elements:

 ## Focus

The *Focus* gives the overall aim of the session.

 ## Scene Setter

The *Scene Setter* gives the Bible passages used for the session, with a key verse pulled out of the text, and background information to help you with your preparation. You will need to familiarize yourself with the whole passage and, in some instances, write it in your own words to relate the story to the group. Other passages can be read with the group from a version of your choice.

 ## Discussion Starters

The *Discussion Starters* are bulleted questions designed to get the group thinking and talking about issues arising from the Bible passage. You might want to develop the discussion along a route highlighted by the group, or add your own questions. Don't forget to include your own experiences in the discussion!

 ## Activities

The *Activities* are designed to explore the theme of the session through the senses and imagination. Some sessions give a range of activities from which to pick those which will suit your group. Some have activities which run over several sessions, building on an ongoing theme, and some have a single activity designed to take up most of the meeting time.

 ## Games

Most of the *Games* can be tailored to work with a group of any size. Some need to be played out-of-doors!

 ## Prayers

The *Prayers* can be used at any point during the session. You might like to ask the children to read them out, or use them as a springboard to write some of your own.

Drawing Together

Drawing Together is a suggestion for an act of worship based on the theme of the session. Many of the suggestions contain simple liturgies using one or two readers and involving the children in antiphonal responses. Do feel free to tailor them to your own situation as you see fit.

The *Prayer* and *Drawing Together* sections of each session are of great importance. They are intended to bring both the people and the work that is done together before God in a way designed to focus on the sacramental aspect of what has been created in the session. This might be through crafts, drama or music. Give the children time to bring their creations to God in worship.

There are a few things to note with some of the specific activities within each of the above elements:

Play Acting

Children will tend to act in a circle facing each other. This is understandable because this is what they do when they talk to each other. When performing a play, however, it is important for them to be aware of the audience. If there is no audience, then suggest one with a couple of rows of chairs.

Photography

A Polaroid camera is a handy asset which will enable you to approach a subject from an unexpected and interesting angle. Many children like to take photographs themselves; this is worth bearing in mind if you wish to use a camera in any of your sessions. Equally entertaining are photographs brought from home, but be aware that there will be those who forget to bring something to the meeting—be prepared by providing 'generic' substitutes for them to use in the activity.

Songs

You will notice that there are no recommendations for songs in the book. This is because there is a wealth of resources available and you are bound to have your favourites. You will find that many of the sessions allow space for singing to be included. If you don't have access to 'live' adult musicians do try to encourage the children to bring their own instruments along. If you wish to use recorded music you will find a wide variety of cassette tapes on the market—or you could even attempt to produce your own.

Don't be afraid to experiment with music and don't worry if the final result isn't quite as polished as professionally produced material. Persistence and practice are all part of the fun!

Outdoor Activities

When embarking on any outdoor activities, ensure that you have experienced and trained people to help you, and check that your church's insurance covers you for the activity you are planning. Never arrange an activity without having checked the safety implications first and advised your minister of your intentions.

Outdoor activities require careful attention to detail. You must have adequate supervision (at least one adult to eight children plus one extra adult if you can manage it) and someone with the relevant qualification if you are planning a sporting activity: for example, someone with lifesaving skills if you are going swimming. You must also obtain the written permission of parents or guardians for each child involved in the activity if you are going off site. Send out a letter giving details of the trip. Include:

★ **The date of the planned activity**

★ **Where you are going**

★ **When you are leaving**

★ **How you are travelling**

★ **Your estimated time of return**

★ **Who the adult helpers are**

★ **Any specific needs, for example, wet weather gear, packed lunch and spending money**

★ **Medical forms if you will be away for the whole day. These should contain details of the child's doctor and any medical information relevant to the activity. Your party should include a named first-aider who is responsible for the child, should an accident occur. The form will need to be**

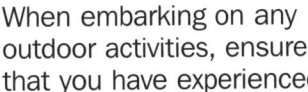

signed by the parent or guardian. Any medicines will need to be put into sealed and labelled bags and handed to the first-aider with instructions for use.

Make a careful check of insurance requirements, especially if using volunteers' cars, which will not usually be insured for the carrying of passengers in this situation. However, with adequate notice, most insurance companies will add the appropriate cover for a small fee.

Finally, make sure you have a basic first-aid kit with you and, if possible, a mobile phone so that you can ring parents or for aid in an emergency.

Outdoor activities need not be daunting or dangerous if you take sensible precautions. Your local council or diocesan office will advise you on the guidelines for planning outdoor activities with children if you are unsure. You should also speak to your minister about any special procedures that your church may require.

Resources

All the resources used in the activities should be readily available from local craft shops, newsagents or DIY stores. It is always worthwhile to maintain a 'junk box' containing scraps of fabric, coloured papers, sweet wrappers, magazines and newspapers, foil and polystyrene containers, card rolls and yogurt pots. All these things will come in handy at some point!

Paper

It is worth bearing in mind that paper doesn't necessarily have to be just A4 sheets. For example, lining paper can be bought cheaply from any DIY store and makes an excellent basis for collages and friezes, and flipchart pads provide a good-sized area for group work.

If you want to mount work, cut the sheets that the children work on before giving them out so that you can use the full sheet as a mount. For example, cut A4 paper down by about 1 cm each side and then use A4 for the mounts. This is much easier than trying to cut small mounts from large sheets.

Scissors

Use scissors that are appropriate to the task and the age or ability of the child. In general it is best to use good sharp scissors as these will cut as desired without forcing the children to use them in a dangerous way—this is especially important when cutting fabrics or stiff card. However, be vigilant in your supervision to ensure that children are using scissors with care.

Modroc

Modroc is bandage impregnated with plaster. It can be obtained from craft shops.

Glues

Glues need to be treated with care. Many of the glues available for children are not suitable for craft activities. However, for most of the activities in this book, a thin layer of PVA (white glue) adhesive will work well, though you may have to apply pressure for a few seconds. If you find that you have to use a solvent-based adhesive, make sure that children are well supervised and that there is adequate ventilation. Rubber solution glue such as Copydex is very good for sticking fabrics. With all gluing activities, access to washing facilities will be required—or at least provide damp cloths for wiping sticky fingers.

Paints

Bear in mind that the quality of paints and colouring pencils will have a direct effect on the results achievable, so buy the best you can afford and keep them in good condition. Clean all your materials carefully after use and replace the lids. You will need a selection of different sized brushes and good quality pencils and crayons. Newspaper and kitchen rolls are also invaluable!

Food

When using food as part of an activity, always pay the strictest attention to hygiene. Supply washing facilities and aprons where necessary and keep all work surfaces scrupulously clean. Ensure you are aware of any allergies which might affect individual members of your group.

Some of the more complex projects, such as the cross sculpture on page 86, will need careful attention and perhaps extra help with the construction. This should provide you with the opportunity to involve others from the congregation in the children's work and the results should be well worth the effort!

Christmas

TERM

Creation

Focus

This session aims to explore one or two aspects of creation in more depth, with particular reference to our emotional response to the created order. Do we feel grateful, excited, happy or sad?

The children are also encouraged to create for themselves—to put themselves in God's shoes! What does it feel like to have created something? How much care and attention went into it? Older children should be encouraged to consider the relationships between the things in their creations.

This is where we started our adventures, at the beginning of Footsteps and Fingerprints; the first Livewires book.

Scene Setter

You need to prepare for the session by reading the whole of the story of creation in Genesis. It is, however, too long to be used in its entirety with the children. Most paraphrased versions seem to rush into the creation of Adam and Eve a little too quickly. Our aim in this session is to extend the appreciation of God's creative work in the making of the world. Genesis 1:1–26 and 31 would therefore provide a suitable abridgment, covering all the creative work of God (apart from the seventh day rest). While you are reading the passage, encourage the group to join in the refrains: '...it was good...' and '...evening and morning came...'. You may wish to use a dramatized version of the Bible.

GENESIS 1:1—2:4

God looked at everything he had made, and he was very pleased.

Discussion Starters

Ask the group to think of things they have made themselves and then encourage them to share some examples. Encourage them to reflect on the feelings associated with these 'creations'. Include your own experiences in the discussion in order to promote a sense of sharing.

- **What do you feel about things that you have made?**
- **What do you feel about how other people treat the things that you have made?**
- **How do you feel about the things that others make?**

Activities

Making shoebox worlds

Grown-ups often say that children are in a world of their own—so here's an opportunity to see what it looks like!

You'll need a small box for each member of the group; shoeboxes are good for this, but almost any box will do. You'll also need plain card, pens, paints, pencils etc., glue and scissors.

Split the group into smaller groups of three or four. The object of the activity is to make a 'scene' in the box. This scene represents the world that the children have created.

When the scene is completed, it then needs things in it that will live together! (Trees, plants animals etc.) They can be 'real' or imaginary. The finished box should have something of the quality of a controlled ecosystem, like a fish-tank.

Encourage the group to exercise their imaginations, but dissuade them from merely copying caricatures and cartoons from TV programmes. Some children may wish to create an undersea scene or an alien planet—these will be harder to achieve effectively, but the results could be quite striking.

When the shoebox worlds are finished, bring everyone together to decide whether each creation is self-sustaining. For example, how are food and water to be provided? Encourage discussion of the merits or pitfalls of each creation.

Younger children may simply want to make a copy of the real world as it is, but make it perfect by, for example, missing out all the fierce animals. Older children can be guided to create imaginary creatures and landscapes of their own. It is important to encourage the group to make choices about their 'worlds' and be aware of their own role in the world's creation. Everyone should be encouraged to have a sense of pride in what they are creating.

Weaving the web of life

You'll need card, pens, paints, pencils etc., rulers and scissors.

This activity helps us to think about the way in which the created world fits together.

Invite everyone to draw a picture of the world, either the earth, or the sea or the sky, but without any living things, on a piece of paper not larger than A4. When they have completed their drawing, fold the paper in half and cut it into strips, leaving a 1–2 cm boundary as shown in the diagram.

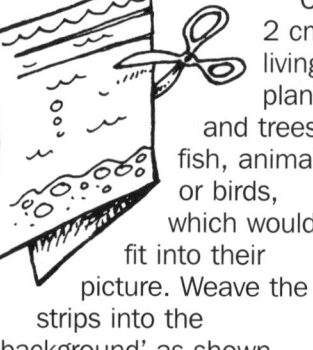

Cut strips of paper about 2 cm wide and draw the living things on the strips: plants and trees, fish, animals or birds, which would fit into their picture. Weave the strips into the 'background' as shown.

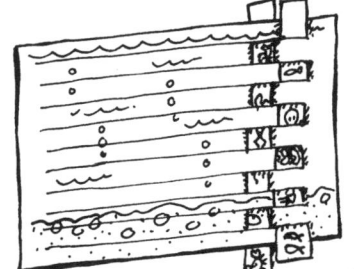

Boot has some suggestions on his factfile of other Bible passages that might be helpful when doing these activities.

An understanding of the world that God created developed very slowly. As the Bible's history unfolds we see a growing awareness of who God is, from the family of Abraham through the judges, kings and prophets to the words of Jesus and the apostles. As people's understanding of God grew, so the understanding of the created world grew as well.

Job 38 and 39 show God's closeness to the world; then chapters 40 and 41 show the power of the created world in the two monsters, Behemoth and Leviathan, whom only God can master: the power of 'nature' is the power of creation.

Older children would enjoy trying to work out what these two creatures are. There have been many theories over the years.

The harvest images in the book of Joel give us a picture of a God in control of the world. These images are in Joel 2:18—3:18, but it is worth reading all of the book of Joel to see how these images fit into the picture of God's power. In Joel's prophecy God is shown as not only providing for the material needs of his people, but also sharing his grace and love. This is perhaps most clear in the famous verses in chapter 2:28–29. This picture of God is clearly mirrored in Paul's words in Acts 14:15–17.

And... don't forget: God's control of all the natural world is strikingly clear in the plagues that were the forerunners of the escape from Egypt. These are to be found in Exodus 7 onwards and give an indication of God's power not only over the natural world but, ultimately, over life and death.

Drama and Dance

Creation provides a good stimulus for a 'cumulative tableau' mime where all the elements are assembled slowly throughout a narration or to a background of music. Here are some suggestions:

⚙ **A picture of Eden can be built up with the group being the creatures and plants. If you are very ambitious you might like to dress everyone up in costumes! If not, simple masks can be made—paper plates provide a good basis for a mask, or, if you want to achieve more 'polished' results, many shops sell animal mask kits which can be easily adapted.**

⚙ **To create the narration, write your own versions of the Genesis account used in the Bible story.**

⚙ **The story of creation or a 'creation' poem could be written by the children and then performed as a tableau to music. Choose appropriate, but not stereotypical, music, for example 'Tattoo' from Mike Oldfield's *Tubular Bells II*.**

⚙ **Organize a creative dance and music workshop where small groups, using short rhythmic pieces, compose their own character dances for a creation ballet: a dance of the fish, or the stars, or the trees, for example.**

⚙ **The national curriculum will have introduced this age group to simple music composition. Your group could use their own instruments, or you could provide simple percussion instruments.**

⚙ **Fictional versions of the creation story would lend themselves to drama and dance. Aslan's song of creation from C.S. Lewis's *The Magician's Nephew* (chapter 9) is a good example. It works well as a reading if you miss out all the 'witch' references.**

⚙ **If you use recorded music for a dance activity, try to find music that is not clichéd—don't use Saint-Saens' *Carnival of the Animals*, for example. Don't be afraid to use modern music; your group may want to suggest something themselves.**

Games

Cotton-reel towers

Empty cotton-reels are best for this game, but you could use card tubes, matchboxes etc. Split the group into small teams, or play the game individually. The object of the game is to see who can make the highest tower in 30 seconds.

A magazine world

> I like this game. It doesn't have to be a competition—it could be used as a collage activity, as well as a game.

Split the group into teams of two or three. From a pile of magazines, each team has to assemble a collage containing pictures of a selection of things mentioned in the creation story—for example, a fish, the moon, the sun, a tree, a man and a woman, a bird, a fruit and a wild animal.

The first team to get them all is the winner.

Prayers

Dear Lord,
Be with us all as we live in your world.
Help us to be aware of all that it contains...
  The good
    The bad
      The sad
        The happy.
Help us to see each part of it with your eyes of love so that we know when...
  To help
    To pray
      To cry
        To laugh.
Help us to love your world. Amen

Heavenly Father,
Be with us as we live in
your world.
Help us to look after it as
if it were our own. **Amen**

Dear Lord,
Thank you for the world,
for its loudness and its quietness,
for its smiles and its tears,
for the part of the world I know and for
the parts known by others.
Thank you for the world. **Amen**

Lord Jesus,
We remember what you did for
this world:
we remember that you came and
lived in it,
we remember that you taught and
healed and laughed in it,
we remember that you wept and you
died in it,
we remember that you rose again in it.
Lord Jesus,
Help us never to forget! **Amen**

Drawing Together

This liturgy works well with people of all ages and could perhaps be used in a family service.

Bringing the world to God

Set up a table with two boxes, one of natural objects—pebbles, wood, plants, feathers, food, etc.—and one of man-made objects—books, toys, china, fabric, etc. (You could arrange for the children to bring these.) Set up a separate table at the front of the room.

Have a procession involving as many of the group as possible. Music should be played throughout the procession.

As the procession moves along, invite everyone to pick out one object from the boxes and set it on the table at the front of the room.

Pick out some of the objects and use the following responses:

Who made the pebbles and stones?
God, our Father, made them all

Who made the plants?
God, our Father, made them all

Who made the trees?
God, our Father, made them all

Reading

PSALM 33:6–9

The Lord created the heavens by his command, the sun, moon, and stars by his spoken word. He gathered all the seas into one place; he shut up the ocean depths in storerooms.

Worship the Lord, all the earth! Honour him, all peoples of the world! When he spoke, the world was created; at his command everything appeared.

Pick out some of the man-made objects on the table and use the following responses:

People made this book
And God made the people

People made this toy
And God made the people

People made this cup
And God made the people

Finish the act of worship with a grace.

Brotherly love

Focus

This session aims to explore some of the themes of Joseph's early life and the events which led up to his being sent to Egypt. We will be looking at the place of Joseph in his own family and linking that to our place in our own families.

We met Joseph right at the beginning of our adventures in Families and Feelings.

Yep! Pages 3–10.

Scene Setter

GENESIS 37:1–11

Jacob loved Joseph more than all his other sons, because he had been born to him when he was old... Joseph's brothers were jealous of him.

This passage emphasizes the tensions in the family. They might appear more obvious in Joseph's family than in our own, but they provide a springboard for us to explore our own family relationships. Joseph is an odd figure in many ways. His manner is seen to be overbearingly precocious with his brothers, yet he was blessed with a sense of God's purpose and presence which never left him.

Discussion Starters

You will need to be sensitive to individual family situations within your group as you explore these questions. The main objective is to focus on how the Bible story ties in to our own lives. What do we learn about ourselves from this passage?

★ What leads to tension in my family?

★ Have I ever had a dream that might have been upsetting to someone else?

★ What would it have been like to be Joseph?

★ What would it have been like to be one of Joseph's brothers?

★ What kinds of things make me jealous?

Activities

Making a family mobile

I enjoyed making these mobiles at my Tuesday Club.

You'll find Joseph's family tree on page 4 of Families and Feelings.

You'll need sheets of thin card, glue, drawing and painting materials, strong thread, thin sticks or straws and scissors.

Using the template overleaf, pre-cut the figures for younger children. Older children might wish to make their own.

GENESIS 35:22–26

Jacob had twelve sons. The sons of Leah were Reuben (Jacob's eldest son), Simeon, Levi, Judah, Issachar, and Zebulun. The sons of Rachel were Joseph and Benjamin. The sons of Rachel's slave Bilhah were Dan and Naphtali. The sons of Leah's slave Zilpah were Gad and Asher.

You could start the tree with Abraham, Isaac, Esau and Jacob. Older children might like to add the children of Joseph—Manasseh and Ephraim.

GENESIS 41:50

Joseph had two sons...
he named his first son
Manasseh... he named his
second son Ephraim.

For each character, cut out two figure shapes and stick together with a length of thread in between. Make a crosspiece with the sticks or straws. Hang each figure from the crosspiece to make a mobile.

Ask each child to name the members of their immediate family. Give them two blank circles for each member. Invite them to draw their family members on the circles, using two circles for each member. If they can go back to previous generations, give them two circles for each member of previous generations known to them. Make up the mobile in the same way as Joseph's family mobile. Hang the mobiles to display them.

Multi-coloured coats

You'll need two lollipop sticks
and two circles of card each,
remnants of fabric, scraps of
haberdashery and glue.

Multi-coloured coats can be made from an assortment of brightly coloured fabrics and then used to dress a lollipop stick figure. Let each child choose a remnant for the basic coat. Calculate the size needed depending on the size of the sticks you are using (see diagram). You may need to pre-cut the fabric for younger children. Older children may wish to cut their own. Decorate the coat with scraps of haberdashery—lace, ribbon and buttons, etc.

Glue two circles of card over the top of the stick to make the head. Draw in the features and colour the hair. Cut a small slit in the coat and slip it up the stick. Glue the second stick to make a cross shape, forming the body and arms.

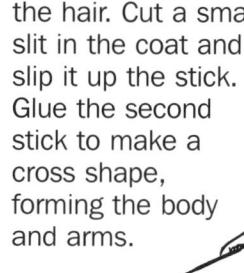

Jacob gave a special coat to Joseph. This was one of the things that made his brothers jealous. What kind of coat was it? What kind of coat might be worn today to show how important someone is?

Digit and I are sometimes jealous of each other—particularly if one of us gets a present or a special surprise and the other one doesn't.

Yeah, that's why we need to remember God's love is special for each one of us—even sisters!

Prayers

Dear Father God,
Be with us when we are together,
learning about you.
Be with us when we play and laugh together.
Be with us when we part. Amen

Lord Jesus,
Help us all to see that we have our part to play
and that it is easy for us to spoil our activities together
by being selfish, proud or jealous.
Amen

Dear God,
When we have something difficult to say, something that we know might hurt others,
please give us your love and care
so that we will be gentle in what we say and kind in what we do. Amen

Dear Lord,
We thank you for our families,
for our friends
and for everyone we know.
Be with us as we live and work and play in your world
and help us to share your love with others. Amen

Father God,
We know that not all families are happy, not all families are whole.
We pray that you will be with those whose families are hurting or broken
and we ask that you will bring comfort and healing to them. Amen

These prayers can be used in the worship or at any point during the session. For some children the subject of families can raise sensitive issues. Silent prayer might be appropriate if this is the case.

Drawing Together

Prayer mobiles

This is a simple idea which makes prayer 'visible'.

You'll need a brightly coloured piece of fabric or a brightly coloured coat, some circles of coloured card approximately 15 cm in diameter and pencils.

Begin with a prayerful song or some reflective music. Give everyone a circle of card.

Choose someone to read each of the following sentences (or make up your own):

Jacob loved Joseph... and made a long robe with full sleeves for him.

This coat reminds us that our heavenly Father loves us. *(Place coat at front.)*

Like Joseph, we are part of a family.

The whole family of God.

Wherever we are—at home, when we are out, when we are on holiday—we remind each other that we are loved by giving to each other.

Heavenly Father, accept these prayers for our families.

Some of them are 'thank you' prayers.

Some of them are 'asking' prayers.

Some of them are 'sorry' prayers.

We offer each one to you.

Amen

Continue to play some gentle music, or keep silent, whilst everyone writes their prayer on a circle of card. Names don't have to be added—God will know who the prayer is from!

When everyone has written their prayer, invite each child to bring their prayer quietly and put it in the pockets of the coat, or fasten it with sticky tape to the fabric. An atmosphere of quiet thoughtfulness should be maintained while this is being done.

Finish with a prayer everyone knows, such as the Lord's Prayer.

Bible Extension

The story of Joseph occupies half of the book of Genesis. It can be helpful to give an overview of the story by picking out the key events and highlighting them by making a collage or storyboard of Joseph's life. The events highlighted might include:

- ⊚ **Joseph's family**
- ★ **Joseph's dreams**
- ⊚ **Joseph down a well**
- ★ **Joseph sold as a slave**
- ⊚ **Joseph in prison**
- ★ **The wine steward and the baker**
- ⊚ **The king of Egypt's dreams**
- ★ **Joseph's brothers' visit to Egypt**
- ⊚ **Joseph and Benjamin**
- ★ **The missing cup**
- ⊚ **The brothers reunited**
- ★ **Joseph's last words to his people**

The Good News Bible gives clear headings for each of these events. You could split your group into twos and threes so that each group illustrates part of the story, which can then be put together as a whole. This activity could be explored in any art form—dance, drama, mime or illustration.

Theme Extension

Use the family mobiles to explore what happens when we do not pull together as a group.

If one of the figures on the mobile is given more importance (more weight) than the others, then the mobile will not balance. Equally, if one person moves away from the others the whole mobile will be upset.

Discuss how this can happen in our groups—not just in the family, but in our school groups, in our church groups or outside clubs.

This picture can be extended further by making a 'gifts' mobile. Put all of the things that we can do for each other together to make one big mobile of 'Our Club' or 'Sunday School' or whatever is appropriate. The important lesson in this is that the whole thing needs to balance, with everything fitting together. We each have our part to play.

Joseph's Dreams

You can perform the dreams through the medium of dance, drama or mime. Make it as simple or ambitious as you like.

> **Use a musical accompaniment which is slightly unusual, mysterious and 'dreamlike': 'Moonchild's Dream' played by Michaela Petri (BMG Music: RCA 1995), or one of Debussy's preludes, might be suitable.**

Split into small groups. Each group chooses someone to play Joseph. The rest of the group takes the part of stars or sheaves of corn.

First of all, think about what the dreams mean. Break up the parts of each dream and make each into a little scene.

Next, think about the reasons why Joseph's brothers were jealous of him. What kind of responses would the brothers have made to Joseph's dreams? Anger? Impatience? Change the emphasis of the dance, drama or mime to show this.

If you have the opportunity to see or hear the musical of *Joseph and his Amazing Technicolor Dreamcoat* you might be able to lead this into attempting a performance of your own. The story-line in the musical is fairly accurate. The original recorded version (1973, RSO Records) is easier to use with children as it is shorter and not as cluttered up with pastiche and showbiz names as the later version.

The creation of a nation

Focus

This unit aims to develop an understanding of how the Jewish nation grew from the roots formed at the time of Abraham. The many rich themes that stem from the passages about Abraham's life include those of promise, purposeful journeys, trust and belief.

> You'll find the beginning of Abraham's journey with God on pages 11–17 in Footsteps and Fingerprints.

Scene Setter

The Bible passages which contain the stories of Abraham are quite extensive. In this session we will concentrate on Abraham's journey. This forms the central part of the action in which God reveals his promises to Abraham. One of the promises we shall explore is that Abraham will have many descendants.

> **GENESIS 12:1**
>
> The Lord said to Abram, 'Leave your country, your relatives, and your father's home, and go to a land that I am going to show you. I will give you many descendants, and they will become a great nation. I will bless you and make your name famous, so that you will be a blessing.'

Discussion Starters

★ **What would make you go on a long journey?**

  ⦿ The promise of riches?

  ⦿ The promise of glory or fame?

  ⦿ The chance to meet someone that you haven't seen for a long time?

★ **What do you think that Abram felt when God asked him to go on a journey?**

★ **What promises did God make to Abram?**

★ **Why would this have been important?**

Activities
A camping trip with Abram and Sarai

> You'll need large sheets of paper for the map, sheets of thin card for the tents and figures, glue and coloured pens or pencils.

The purpose of this activity is to reinforce the length of the journey undertaken by Abram. The map on page 19 is also on page 17 of *Footsteps and Fingerprints*.

Copy the map on to a large piece of paper (it doesn't have to be perfect!) The bigger you can get it, the better—you might choose to use several pieces of paper joined together, or strips of wallpaper. Lay the map on the floor of your meeting room.

Have your group prepare for the journey by making tents and figures out of card from the templates given. Make at least one item for every child in your group. These will be used to help the group follow the stages of Abram's journey. The journey is told by way of a series of imaginary extracts from Sarai's journal. This provides a summary of the story, with Bible references given to help you follow the outline of the biblical record.

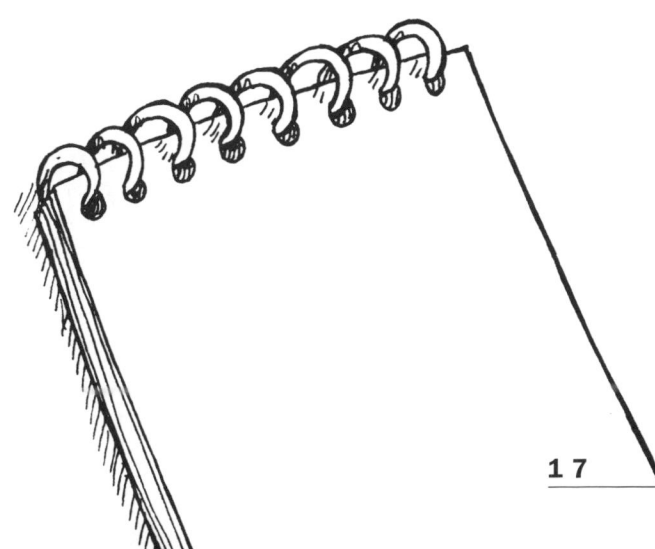

Tuesday. Married Abram today, a nice wedding with all the trimmings. Terah, Abram's dad, is very kind. We have settled down with the family in Ur. I wonder when Abram will want to start a family? (Genesis 11:27–29)

Activity

Find Ur on your map and, reading out the Bible passage, place the figures and a symbol of marriage on the map. The symbol could be drawn or an actual item, such as an inexpensive ring.

🌀 **How old do you think the bride and groom would have been?**

🌀 **Why do you think the Bible mentions the fact that Sarai was not able to have children?**

Activity

Place folded tents on the map in preparation for the journey.

★ **What mode of transport would have been available to Abram?**

★ **Why do you think the family needed to move on?**

Saturday. We've been going for a week now and we are all getting tired. Our son-in-law, Lot, has come with us. He talks non-stop! Terah says that we are going to Haran, which is quite a big town.

Saturday. We've been married for two years now. Abram's dad Terah thinks that we should move the family business north. Abram agrees with him so we are packing up. Abram does want a family—but we've had no luck yet. (Genesis 11: 31–32)

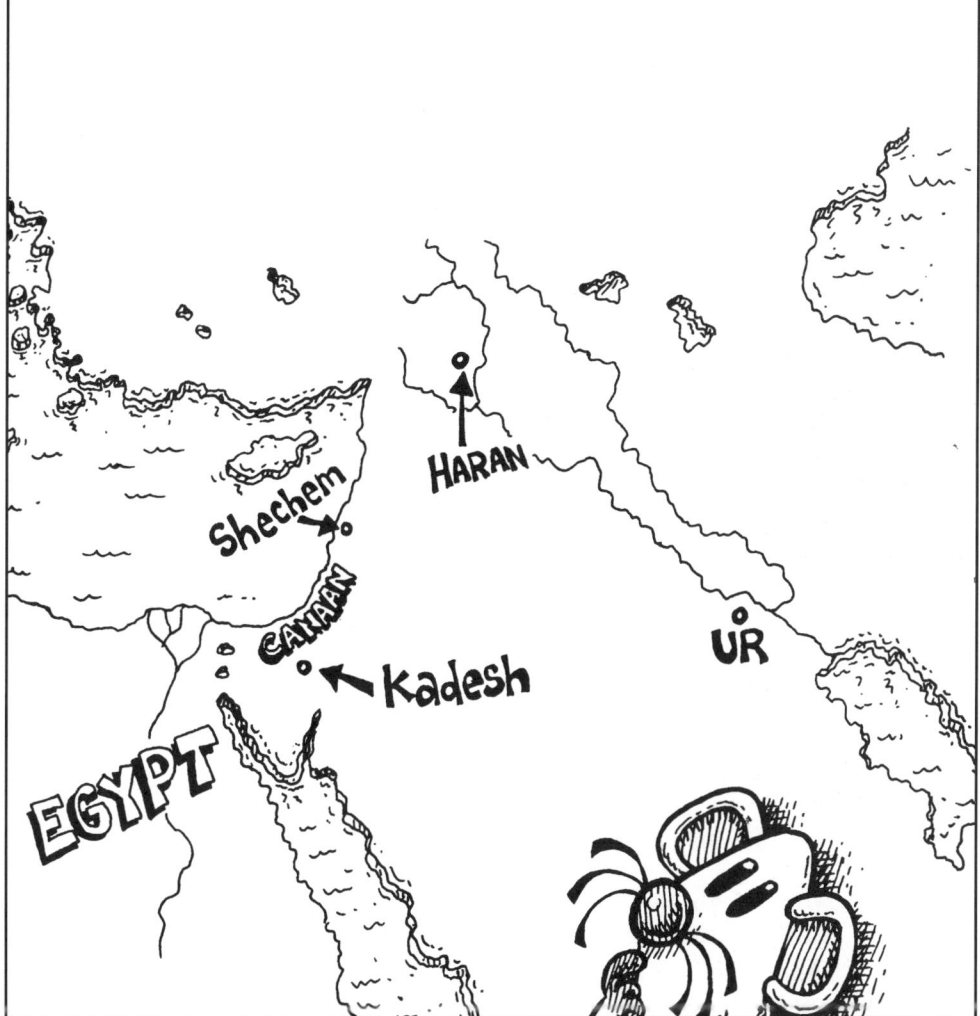

Activity
Find Haran on the map.

 How far do you think it is from Ur to Haran?

 How many miles would they have had to walk each day?

 Can you think of a journey locally which would be a similar distance?

 How long would it take you to walk there?

> As the diary progresses you could add further questions relevant to your group. If you feel that this makes the activity too drawn out, then just follow the journey on the map for the rest of the activity.

Monday. It took ages to get to Haran; there were some pretty big hills to climb. Mind you, the view was pretty amazing.

★ Where is the highest hill you have climbed?

★ What was the view like from the top?

★ How long did it take you to climb up?

★ How long did it take you to come down again?

Friday. We've been here for several years now and today was the strangest of all of them. Abram came to see me this morning and told me that God had spoken to him and that we are to move on. I am not pleased 'cos I thought we could settle down here to raise our family. Anyway, we have to go, and Abram did say that God told him he was going to have many descendants. I'd like a family.
(Genesis 12:1—5)

Tuesday. We've arrived in Canaan, but we have to keep moving around, partly to find food for all the goats that we own. Abram is getting very serious about doing what God says. He built an altar today and we all said prayers round it.
(Genesis 12:6—9)

Wednesday. In the last four months we have moved an awful lot but there is no food—all the land has dried up. Abram and Lot (who came with us from Haran) have decided to go to Egypt to find food. And I was hoping to start that family.
(Genesis 12:10)

Tuesday. We are leaving Egypt in a hurry. Abram has been in trouble with the king. Abram pretended that I was his sister, not his wife, and the king wanted to marry me. When he found out that he couldn't, he told Abram to leave the country. Lot is coming with us as well!
(Genesis 12:17—20)

> Note that Abraham left Haran before Terah died.

Thursday. We are doing better now we are back in Canaan, but that Lot can't keep his servants in order. They keep arguing with Abram's servants. The two men have agreed to separate and Lot is getting all the best land, down by the river. Abram doesn't know what he's doing sometimes. We'll need all the help we can get when we have a baby. (Genesis 13:1–13)

Monday. That Lot will be the end of us. We've only just settled here under some lovely terebinth trees and he gets himself caught up in a battle. Abram has gone off to rescue him. I shall have something to say when he comes back. (Genesis 14:1–21)

Tuesday. Abram is back now and very pleased with himself. He won the battle and rescued Lot. (Genesis 14:22–24)

Friday. Abram says that God spoke to him again and made that promise about children again. It seems that it was all very serious: it was a proper legal promise; Abram calls it a covenant, a real business agreement. He should know, he's been successful in business for ages. (Genesis 15)

Tuesday. I don't think that I'm ever going to have children. I'll suggest that Abraham has another wife; perhaps she can have children. (Genesis 16:1–2)

Saturday. Abram has agreed to my idea. And now my maid, Hagar, is going to have his child. (Genesis 16:3–4)

Monday. We've been having trouble with Hagar—she keeps running away. But she's had her baby; he is called Ishmael. Abram met God again last night. And God told him that I was going to have a baby. Not only that, but apparently we have to change our names. I am to be called Sarah and he will be called Abraham. (Genesis 17)

Wednesday. Abraham was visited by three men today—and they told him that I was going to have a baby as well! I just laughed. (Genesis 18:1–15)

2 1

Friday. We've moved again, to the south of the country. The strangest thing has happened—I'm going to have a baby, and I'm ninety years old! We are going to call the boy Isaac. (Genesis 21)

Games

Follow my leader

You'll need some music— either live or recorded.

This game is a good ice-breaker.

Put the group in pairs. Each pair decides who is going to be the leader. When the music is played the leader moves in time with the music and their partner follows their lead. You can add a variation by getting the children to swap leader/follower role when you blow a whistle.

Amazing mazes

Paper-based mazes

You'll need squared paper, pencils, rulers and compasses.

If you are unsure about designing your own mazes, you'll find plenty of ideas in the Livewires books.

Each child sets out their maze, using the squared paper to ensure that the paths are a consistent width. Older children might want to try creating circular mazes, in which case a pair of compasses will be needed.

If you use compasses it is best to get good metal ones and have the children work on a soft surface such as a magazine.

Marble mazes

You'll need one polystyrene tile and a marble for each child, some pots of strong children's glue, rulers and scissors.

Marble mazes can be made with wood. This, however, can be expensive and requires access to specialist tools. Polystyrene tiles make a good alternative. Before the session, cut a 1 cm strip from each side of each tile, using a Stanley knife. The children then cut the strips to size and stick them on the tile to form the paths for the marble to roll along. Make sure you calculate the width of the paths to allow the marble to travel smoothly.
If you wanted to make a strong link with Abraham you could put small labels along the route of the maze to indicate the various stages of his journey.

Abraham talked to God a lot. When we talk to God we call it prayer. Try talking to God with these prayers.

Prayers

Dear Lord,
Thank you for the things we can
promise to do.
Help us to remember to keep our
promises
so that other people learn to trust us.
And help us to learn to trust you. **Amen**

Heavenly Father,
When we are sad and lonely
help us to remember that we are part
of your great journey
which began with Abraham.
Be with each of us today
as we continue on our own special
journey with you. **Amen**

Dear God,
Help us to remember your promises
whenever we look up at the stars in
the sky, like Abraham did.
Help us to remember your promises
whenever we look at a newborn baby,
like Sarah did.
Help us to remember your promises
whenever we look at Jesus,
like those who have followed you
throughout history did. **Amen**

Drawing Together

Choose someone to read the Bible passages—you might like to type the verses out on separate sheets of paper beforehand.

Ask the children to spread out around the room. They can work singly or in groups of two or three.

Between each reading, the children move and form a picture using their bodies. They represent constellations in the sky. Real stars! If you can provide stage lighting it makes a very impressive performance.

First reader

God said to Abram: 'Leave your country, your relatives, and your father's home, and go to a land that I am going to show you. I will give you many descendants, and they will become a great nation. I will bless you and make your name famous, so that you will be a blessing.'

Genesis 12:1–2

We are the children of God's promise
We are like stars in the sky

Second reader

God said to Abram: 'I am going to give you so many descendants that no one will be able to count them all; it would be as easy to count all the specks of dust on earth!'

Genesis 13:16

We are the children of God's promise
We are like stars in the sky

Third reader

God said to Abram: 'Do not be afraid, Abram. I will shield you from danger and give you a great reward.'

Genesis 15:1

We are the children of God's promise
We are like stars in the sky

Fourth reader

God said to Abram: 'Look at the sky and try to count the stars; you will have as many descendants as that.'

Genesis 15:5

We are the children of God's promise
We are like stars in the sky

Fifth reader

Abraham was patient, and so he received what God had promised... We have this hope as an anchor for our lives.

Hebrews 6:15 and 19

We are the children of God's promise
We are like stars in the sky

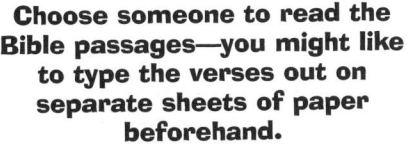

The story of Ruth

Focus

This session is based on the theme of harvest and aims to explore the link between the celebration of the season and our own responsibility to care for our world and those around us.

> You'll find the story of Ruth on pages 11–17 of Families and Feelings.

> In our adventure, Ruth fell in love with Boot! Yuck!

Scene Setter

The story of Ruth provides a romantic interlude between the judges and the kings of the Old Testament. Ruth brings a touch of the reality of human life amongst the quickfire stories of great heroes (and not-so-great heroes) in the books of Judges and Samuel. The story is a bridge in the ancestry of David, demonstrating his links with Abraham, but it also paints cameo pictures of the traditions of the people of Israel as they lived their lives under the Law of Moses. One well-known example of this is the giving of the sandal in chapter 3. The book is closely associated with the season of harvest and is read at harvest-time by Jewish people in the synagogues.

It would be a good idea to read right the way through the book of Ruth in preparation for this session. With only four chapters, it is not too daunting a task! We shall be concentrating on Ruth 2:1–21, but it would be useful to give a resumé of the story, including the following points:

- Set the scene. Ruth is a Moabite woman.
- ★ Naomi travels to Moab with her husband and sons because there is a famine in her native Bethlehem.
- Ruth marries one of Naomi's sons.
- ★ Following the death of her husband, Ruth shows uncommon loyalty, both to her Israelite mother-in-law, Naomi, and to God.
- Naomi and Ruth return to Bethlehem.
- ★ Ruth meets Boaz, who is a relative of Naomi.
- Boaz marries Ruth.
- ★ Ruth and Boaz have a son called Jesse, who becomes the father of David.

Discussion Starters

- In what ways can we share what we have?
- ★ Who would you want to share your things with?
- Who wouldn't you want to share your things with?
- ★ Is there anything that you would want others to share with you?

> ### RUTH 2:3
> So Ruth went out to the fields and walked behind the workers, picking up the corn which they left. It so happened that she was in a field that belonged to Boaz.

Activities
Sharing what we have— a world collage

> You will need a photo of each child in your group, empty food packaging (boxes, wrappers, labels etc.), a selection of colour magazines or news supplements, sheets of plain card or old rolls of wallpaper, glue and safety scissors.

The children need to be photographed in advance, in poses of offering and carrying (not necessarily looking at the camera). If you don't have a camera, then you could ask the children to bring photos of themselves from home. If you have a Polaroid camera you could take everyone's photo as they arrive at the beginning of the session.

You will also need to have collected a selection of pictures of food from magazines or news supplements (look out for recipes), and empty food packaging which could be collected over a series of weeks. Make sure it's all clean! Finally you need magazine pictures of people from all around the world. By planning ahead, the children will be able to make their own collections of all the items over the weeks leading up to the session.

Split the group into twos and threes or, if the group is quite small, work together using a length of wallpaper as the backing for the collage. Explain that the collage needs to reflect the story of Ruth 2:1–21, where Boaz shares his plenty with those around him.

The whole collage should end up showing the children themselves sharing what they have with those around them. This is a significant point in the story of Ruth. Boaz did not just allow her to glean (by law he could not have stopped that) but he invited her to eat with him as well. This might have been because he was attracted to her, but equally it might have been because she was Naomi's daughter-in-law, and therefore a member of his own family. Boaz took the trouble to find out who Ruth was and to act accordingly. How might we follow his example to help those less fortunate than ourselves?

God our provider

> **ACTS 14:17**
>
> '...he gives you rain from heaven and crops at the right times; he gives you food and fills your hearts with happiness.'

The aim of this activity is to show all that God does for us in providing the harvest. Start the activity by discussing what things God gives us to make the harvest. These things can be depicted in the following ways:

- By painting examples of all those things which contribute to the harvest (rain, sun, soil, seeds etc.) and displaying the pictures around the room
- By cutting items from magazines and catalogues and assembling them into a collage
- By gathering items from real life, for example, a jar of rainwater, a cup of seeds, a small amount of soil etc. The items could then be displayed together on a table

Write out the passage from Acts in full, or simply the key phrases from it, and put it with your display.

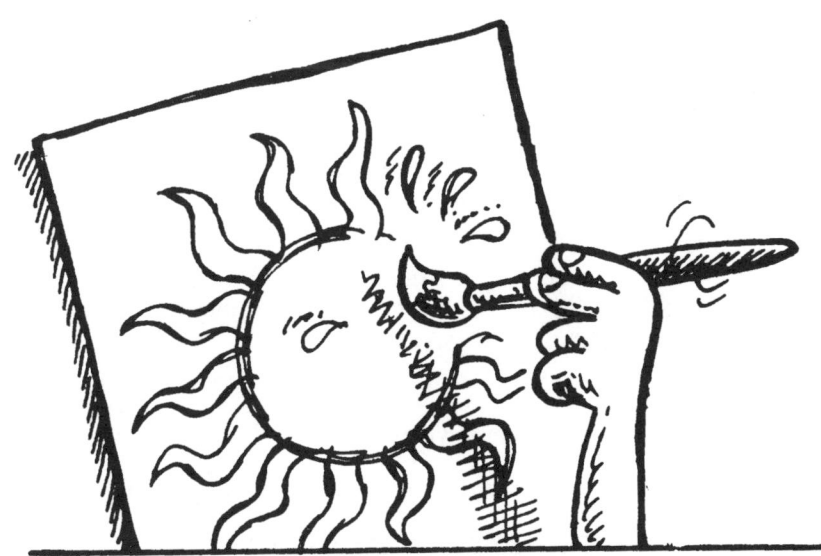

Prayers

Dear Lord,
You are Lord of the harvest.
It is your gift to us.
Help us to share this gift to help others,
just as Ruth helped Naomi,
and Boaz helped Ruth. Amen

Almighty God,
We are your children and meet together
to enjoy being with each other and with
you.
Be with us as we learn together
about all the wonderful things you have
given us. Amen

Father God,
Thank you for your gifts to us all.
The gift of food and water.
The gift of metal and wood.
The gift of love and care.
Help us to learn how to use all these
things wisely,
in Jesus' name. Amen

Worship

Gathering and gleaning—
a harvest celebration

You will need a selection of foods (one item per child, all of which will be given to the smaller group in the middle of the circle).

Choose one person to be the reader and divide the rest of the group in two: a smaller group who sit close together with all the food items and a larger group who make a circle round them.

Reader

We live in an age of plenty, there is food for us all.

Larger group

Yet we are hungry.

Reader

Look, we have... and... (pick different food items from the smaller group and name them).

Larger group

Yet we are hungry.

Reader

We give a little away (push one or two items out towards the larger group).

Larger group

Yet we are hungry.

Reader

We throw food away (again, push a couple of things out).

Larger group

Yet we are hungry.

Reader

The hungry look on as the few eat and drink. They can only have a little of what there is.

Smaller group

What can we do?

Reader

Learn from Boaz. Look around you at the need of others. Invite them to come and share your plenty.

The central group hands out the items of food until everybody has something.

Close with the Lord's Prayer and a song of your choice.

Game

Gatherers and gleaners

This is a team game, based on It's a Knock-Out.

You will need two buckets and a large bag of uncooked rice per team. The floor needs to be marked into lanes with chalk or rope and the buckets placed at either end of the lane. Each lane is a 'field'. The object of the game is for each team to get their rice from the first bucket to the second, using only their hands to transport it. Each team chooses one member to be a gleaner.

The gleaner can collect rice that other teams have dropped by visiting the other teams' fields. The gleaner cannot pick up rice from their own field. The team with the most rice in the second bucket at the end of the game is the winner. Each team stands in a line behind their first bucket. The first person in the line grabs a handful of rice, runs to put it into the second bucket and runs back again to tag the next team member, who then takes their turn. You can either set a time limit, or agree on a set number of turns to be taken by each team member before the game ends.

Theme extension

Split the group into three teams and give each team as many Bibles as you can. Ask each team to look up one of the following passages:

LEVITICUS 19:9–10,
DEUTERONOMY 24:19–22,
LEVITICUS 19:33–34

Ask each team to read out their passage. Where does this law fit into the story of Ruth?

Next, ask each team to look up one of the following passages:

EXODUS 23:14–15,
EXODUS 23:16,
EXODUS 23:17

⊚ How many festivals are celebrated in this passage?

★ Why are they celebrated?

⊚ How does our own celebration of harvest differ from the Hebrew festivals?

★ In what ways is it similar?

Belonging

Focus

This session aims to develop an understanding of how we fit into the picture of creation.

You'll find this theme on pages 39–44 of Families and Feelings.

Scene Setter

The Bible paints a picture of humans being part of creation within the context of the kingdom of God, with God as the king. We belong to God because we are in the world, and also in his kingdom. By the same token God is *our* God; there is a sense in which God also belongs to us.

PSALM 24

The world and all that is in it belong to the Lord; the earth and all who live on it are his.

This short psalm is full of exciting images and powerful poetic elements. The opening verses of the psalm celebrate God's creation of the natural world. Verse 2 reflects the ancient belief that the world was saucer-shaped. The use of repeated phrases in verses 7–10 would have been antiphonal, with the choir outside the gate asking, 'Who is this great king?' and the priests within replying, 'He is the Lord, strong and mighty... the triumphant Lord, he is the great king!' This striking emphasis draws the reader/hearer into the triumphant celebration of the psalm: 'Fling wide the gates, open the ancient doors, and the great king will come in.'

Discussion Starters

As you explore the theme through these questions, encourage the children to be honest about how they feel. If you too are honest about your own feelings, this will be an encouragement to them. Make sure they know that anything they say won't go outside the group.

- ⊚ Who does each one of us belong to?
- ★ What does this mean to you?
- ⊚ What about other members of your family? Who do they belong to?
- ★ What about us as a nation? Where do people like the Queen or the Prime Minister fit in?
- ⊚ Why does the psalmist say that we belong to God?
- ★ Do you feel that you belong in the church?
- ⊚ Does the church belong to you?

Activities

An autumn country walk

If you live near a park, this would be the ideal place to go, or you could organize a trip out if you live in a town or city.

Give plenty of advance warning that you will be going out so that you can enlist help, sort out safety procedures and ensure the children know to bring bags to make their collections in.

You'll find safety guidelines in the Introduction.

You'll need small bags, small notepads of plain paper and pencils.

As you walk along, look out for things that 'belong': leaves on the trees, fruit on the ground and so on. Gather small items to use back at your base. There are some things you might see that 'belong', like animal tracks, which you cannot take back with you. These could either be noted, or drawings made of them.

Enjoy the walk. Try to encourage the children to be observant. Some of them may be more familiar with the area than you are and be able to supply extra information about the locality.

Here are some suggestions for using the objects you have gathered.

Autumn plate gardens

You'll need paper plates and a small quantity of damp sand.

Create the gardens from pebbles, twigs and leaves etc. Encourage the children to use their imaginations to show how different objects belong together and have been part of something else, for example, a plant in a wood.

Autumn pictures

You'll need sheets of thin, coloured card and cow-gum type glue.

Put the children into groups of three or four. Each group chooses a backing colour onto which to arrange the objects that they have collected. These are then glued in place to form pictures. The pictures can be actual images, abstract or patterns. Allow the children to choose. If the children use flat objects—leaves, feathers, petals etc.—then the pictures could be mounted into clip-frames, which make very professional-looking semi-permanent displays.

Make sure you get clip-frames with safety glass.

Printing

You'll need sheets of thin card and a selection of poster paints.

Many of the objects that the children find can be used as printing blocks. Thick veined leaves and thin strips of bark both work well. Use quite thick paint. Carefully spread it over the object and lay it

down gently on the paper. Try not to slide it as you lift it off. You can experiment with different colours. If you don't have enough leaves to use a fresh one each time, they can be washed. Experiment with different pressures to obtain different effects and try sliding objects to create a variety of patterns and shapes.

Sculptures

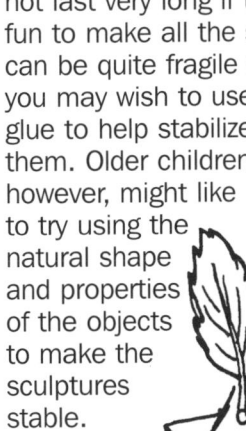

You'll need thick card for the base and some strong glue.

Bulky objects, such as fruit, wood and animal bones, can be assembled into sculptures. These will not last very long if they include fruit, but they are fun to make all the same. They can be quite fragile so you may wish to use glue to help stabilize them. Older children, however, might like to try using the natural shape and properties of the objects to make the sculptures stable.

Talk about the work. Try to bring out that the things that everyone has collected belong to God in the same way that we do, and that they grow and change just as we do. You might like to lead the discussion into the concept of new growth from the seeds and the life-cycle of natural objects. This is all part of belonging to God—including our own life-cycle!

Even when we have arguments we are glad that we belong together... and that we belong to God. Sometimes we pray about it. Here are some of our favourite prayers.

Prayers

Heavenly Father,
On our walk we have seen
many things you have created.
Thank you that you have made all
things to fit together.
Thank you for the special place
of belonging
that you have given us in your world.
Amen

Dear God,
Thank you that we belong together
as part of your family.
Be with us through our good times
and our bad times.
Be with us as we learn more about
ourselves,
about each other and about you. *Amen*

Father God,
We pray for all the clubs and classes
that we belong to,
for all the things we do there
and for all the people that we meet.
We ask you to help us to play our
full part
so that others will see that we
really belong. *Amen*

Games

> If you have collected conkers, acorns or beech nuts on your walk you could use them to play one of the following games.

Animal noises

> You'll need a large quantity of conkers, or something similar, and a small container for each team.

Put the conkers in piles around the room. Split the group into teams and give each team the name of an animal: sheep, cows, pigs, cats, chickens etc.

Give the team leader the container. Only the team leader can collect the conkers. The team members run to a pile and call their team leader over by making the noise of their team's animal. The winning team is the one with the fullest container once all the conkers have been gathered.

If you are able to play this game out-of-doors, you will be able to distribute the conkers over a much wider area!

Dance

Crack and gleam

> You'll need a small straight stick, about 70 cm long, for each child.

> I love dancing, so I love this game! For music see page 124.

This little tune is danced to in the style of a Morris dance. The tune can be played on any instrument—use the talents of your group where possible. A simple drum sound could be added.

The children stand in pairs, forming two circles around one central person who is the 'tree'. Each child holds a short stick.

Using a simple left, left, right, right step, the children dance around the tree, first to the left and then to the right. In the second part of the tune (bars 5–8), the 'tree' raises his/her stick and the rest of the dancers use their sticks as follows:

Bar 5

One person of each pair taps their partner's stick for three beats, then they both step in toward the 'tree'.

Bar 6

Each dancer taps the tree's stick for three beats, then steps out again.

Bar 7

As Bar 5

Bar 8

As Bar 6

The dance then starts again at the beginning and is continued for three or four rounds.

In order to avoid bruised knuckles, the dancers need to ensure that their strikes are very gentle.

You might want to add your own variations to the dance once you have learnt the basic steps.

Drawing Together

Draw the session together in a celebration of the kingship of God and our place in his kingdom.

> **You'll need a small wooden cross, a crown, either home-made or from a toy shop, and a length of plain material, preferably purple.**

Start the worship either with a song or by playing some music. Form a procession in pairs. Choose three people to bring the cross, the crown and the purple robe to the front. The rest of the group chooses an item from the collection of natural objects to bring.

1st person   I bring a cross, the emblem of our king.

2nd person   I bring a crown, the emblem of our king.

3rd person   I bring a royal robe, the emblem of our king.

Arrange each item as it is brought to the front and continue with a song or music.

Invite each child to bring one of the treasures that they found on the walk to the front.

Child   I bring a ..., the emblem of our king.

Sit quietly, playing music if you wish.

Finish with a prayer.

In this worship it is important that *any* natural object is an emblem of God, our king.

Theme extension

You may wish to extend the theme by looking at how the understanding of the place of historical kings and queens has contributed to our images of God as king. This can be both through the biblical records and through our own national history. Link the exploration in to how God has been portrayed in art as king with, for instance, images of rich clothes and haloes.

Lead this in to looking at the ways that Christ has been portrayed as king. You might know of a church, for example, which has been named Christ the King. Look at the way that Matthew shows Jesus as a king at the beginning of his Gospel.

Invite the children to discuss their own image of Jesus. You could do this verbally, or through art. What would be their emphasis of him in their own picture?

Calendar Link

Although this theme is not strictly for harvest, you could use it to link in to the season of harvest if you wished. Create a sense of expectation and preparation. What are our expectations of harvest? Why? What are we preparing for? What do trees and plants prepare for at this time of year? How?

Parables of Jesus

Focus

The aim of this session is to explore what type of stories the parables of Jesus are, and what they teach us about Jesus and about ourselves.

We met a travelling storyteller on pages 25–31 of Families and Feelings.

He told us some really cool stories!

Scene Setter

The stories Jesus told teach us about God's kingdom and about ourselves, but sometimes they also hide their meaning. Sometimes the meaning is deliberately hidden from the *original* hearers and sometimes it is hidden from us because we are coming to the stories so long after their original telling. When we read the parables of Jesus we are looking back across 2000 years and it is not always easy to understand the original context in which they were told.

LUKE 8:9–10

His disciples asked Jesus what this parable meant, and he answered, 'The knowledge of the secrets of the Kingdom of God has been given to you, but to the rest it comes by means of parables, so that they may look but not see, and listen but not understand.'

Discussion Starters

★ In what ways could you hide the meaning of what you were saying from someone?

★ What would you do if you wanted some people to understand what you were saying but not others?

★ What kinds of stories do you remember easily?

★ What is your favourite story?

★ If you were going to tell a story, what would it be about?

Activities

Split the group into small teams of three of four.

You will need at least one Bible per team, sheets of paper and pencils.

Give one of the following parables to each team:

LUKE 18:9–14, MARK 4:26–29, LUKE 12:16–21, LUKE 15:1–6

The parables can be explored in one of the following ways:

@ Ask each team to find and read the passage together. They then have to either make up their own version of the parable, or tell it in their own words. Once they have done this they recite their parable to the rest of the group. Encourage them to be as imaginative as possible. They need to look carefully at the different characters involved and to imagine what they would have said and what their feelings would have been. Try to ensure that everyone contributes to the activity.

⑥ Choose one of the parables and discuss it together. Who is involved? What do they do? What is the story teaching us? Is there anything that is being hidden from the original hearer? Is there anything we don't understand about the parable? When the group is familiar with the parable, act it out as a drama or a mime. Use those who haven't got main parts as the crowd or the disciples. How did the crowd react to Jesus' parables? How did the disciples?

⑥ Collect together a large selection of magazines. Split the group into twos or threes. Give each small group a Bible and ask them to look up one of the parables of your choice. When they have read the parable together, ask them to cut out pictures in the magazines which remind them of the events or characters in the story. The pictures can either be made up as a collage in the small groups, using sheets of card as a backing, or all the groups could contribute to one large collage, using a length of wallpaper as the backing.

Illustrating the parables with puppets

LUKE 10:25-37

...the teacher of the Law asked Jesus, 'Who is my neighbour?'

First of all, read the parable to the group. You could use a children's version of the story if you prefer. Like all parables, this one had an audience but, unlike most of the parables, we know something about who was listening to it. We are told that Jesus told the parable to the teacher of the Law. Jesus and the teacher provide the frame through which the story is played out, so the puppetry could be performed as if these two characters were watching it.

The puppets

One of the most exciting aspects of a puppet show is making the puppets in the first place. There are many ways to do this (you may know of several), but here is a suggestion:

You will need a selection of kitchen utensils: wooden spoons, wooden salad forks, spatulas or slotted spoons would all be suitable. You'll also need enamel paint or marker pens, scraps of fabric for clothes, scissors, glue and a large box or cloth to form the 'stage'.

Salad forks have great hair!

Split the group into twos or threes to make the puppets. Provide plenty of newspaper if you have decided to use paint, or simply use marker pens to make the puppets' features. Cut simple conical cloaks from the scraps of fabric and glue them to the 'neck' of each puppet. Once the puppets are made you can either write a script for the puppets, or just use the puppets to illustrate the story as it is read out. This is probably easier to begin with.

Set up the box or cloth to provide a 'stage' for the performance. Don't forget the characters of Jesus and the teacher of the Law!

Prayers
Heavenly Father,
Thank you for stories.
For the stories we tell and
the stories we hear.
For the stories we write and the stories
we read.
And thank you most of all for your story
which we find in the Bible. Amen

Dear Lord,
We praise you for the
things that you have given
us,
especially for the things that teach us.
Help us to understand the stories that
Jesus told
and to share them with others. Amen

Drawing Together

LUKE 15:1–32

A celebration of the God who runs with open arms to bring us home

You'll need some items to represent the things that can make us forget about God; for example, a video tape, some money, a football and a computer game. You'll also need some small cakes and balloons.

Start by explaining that none of the items you've chosen is bad in itself, it's just the way we use them which makes them become a barrier between us and God. For example, watching videos which glamorize violence, hankering after being very rich, playing sport or computer games excessively, etc. Put the children into small groups and sit them in a circle on the floor. Put a cloth in the centre of the circle and give each group one of the items. Put the cakes and balloons on a table to one side of the room. Choose a reader to read out each sentence as you move through the liturgy.

Reader	Jesus taught us many things about God.
First group	Forgive us when we forget the things he taught us. (They put their item on the cloth.)
Reader	Jesus taught us how to find the kingdom of God.

Second group	Forgive us when we forget to follow the path. (They put their item on the cloth.)
Reader	Jesus taught us how to behave towards our neighbours.
Third group	Forgive us when we do not treat others fairly. (They put their item on the cloth.)
Reader	Jesus taught us how to praise him.
Fourth group	Forgive us when we forget to praise you, Lord. (They put their item on the cloth.)
Reader	God runs to meet us with open arms.

Gather up the cloth with the items inside it. Set the cakes and balloons out in the middle of the circle.

All	Come and join the party!

Finish by saying the Lord's Prayer together and by singing a song of your choice. Finally, distribute the cakes and balloons to everyone.

Fingerprints

Focus

This section explores the senses as ways into experiencing God's world. We are made as beings with senses and we often deny their importance in our lives, but when we read the Bible we find all of the senses are given their full respect: Jesus touching, Elijah hearing, even Lazarus' family smelling!

> I had lots of fun with senses—when the Livewires were asleep!

> I wasn't asleep—look in Footsteps and Fingerprints, page 37.

Scene Setter
The healing of the blind man

> MARK 8:22–25
>
> Jesus placed his hands on him and asked him, 'Can you see anything?'

This passage has been chosen because of the 'half-healing' which takes place and what the man says about trees walking about. This process of the miracle reveals something of the property of sight with which Jesus could identify. This holds true for all the senses: while the sensations are more or less private in themselves, we all know what those sensations are like. It is through this sharedness that Jesus was able to identify that the man's sight was not completely healed the first time.

Discussion Starters

Think about senses and about the information that they give us.

◎ **What kinds of things do our senses tell us?**

◎ **Are they ever wrong?**

◎ **Do we all agree about what our senses are telling us?**

Activities

Different sights

Making 'eyes-closed pictures'

> Drawing is something that I love—you might have seen my sketches in the Livewires books—but painting is even better. This is a painting activity that is so cool you'll freeze!

> You will need paper (black works well in this activity), paint, brushes and at least two reading-lamps.

This activity needs to be set up with some care, so that everyone understands what they are to do. The basic idea is that you:

1. **Look at a brightly lit area.**

2. **Close eyes tight.**

3. **Draw/paint what you see when your eyes are closed.**

Light up a portion of a wall with the reading-lamps. Overlap the patches of light to make bright and dark areas. You could use coloured bulbs if you wished, or add a spotlight bulb to give a very bright area.

Paint is by far the best medium for this activity as results can be achieved very quickly.

Invite your group to look at the lit area for a moment (while you count ten, say) and then close their eyes. They then open their eyes and think about what they saw when their eyes were closed. This is not easy because the image changes when the eyes are re-opened. It is probably best to do the look/close-eyes part of the activity a few times before moving on to painting. Talk about the fact that we may see the same image, but with colour reversed. For example, red becomes green when the eyes are closed. This activity is expressive and immediate. Children should not see 'recognizable' images such as TV characters etc; if they say they see these, encourage them to remember what they saw as *patterns and colours*, not what it makes them think of.

It may be appropriate to do this activity several times in order to allow the group to get used to the idea of what they are doing.

The finished paintings will be very personal. Each one will be an 'eyeprint', unique in the same way as a fingerprint. This being so, give the group the option to take their pictures home. The paintings would, however, make a very nice display if the children so wished.

Making illusions

Making illusions is an art activity. Artists who use this form include Escher and Vasarely.

Illusions are fun; if you can get hold of any Escher prints, these will fascinate the children. Talk about how we interpret illusions and invite the children to draw illusions of their own.

> There are some simple illusions in Footsteps and Fingerprints. However, don't ask the children to copy those, let them try to develop their own illusions.

The most common illusion used in art is, of course, perspective, where we are led to believe that a flat canvas has depth. The children might like to experiment with perspective effects.

Prayers

Dear Lord,
We are all different,
even to our fingertips.
Help us to remember that you make
each one of us special
and, even though we are different,
you love us all with the same love.
Amen

Our Father,
Be with us in your world,
when we smell the plants,
when we hear the birds,
when we taste the fruits,
when we see the sky,
and when we touch the grass;
because in doing these things we are
drawing close to you.
Amen

Theme Extension

Exploring the senses— build a Senseum

A Senseum is a museum of the senses, where you not only see unusual things but can also smell, taste, touch and hear things. It is constructed as follows:

> You will need cloth, elastic, paint, paper, scissors, pencils, crisps, audio cassettes, a tape recorder, microphone and an assortment of everyday objects.

Feely bags

Stitch three sides of two fabric squares together and turn the bag inside out. Either make a hem at the top of the bag or make holes to thread 8–10 cm of elastic through. Tie off the elastic to secure. Invite the group to put objects into the bags. Visitors (parents) then have to guess what the objects are.

Orange to red illusion

Start by mixing a yellowy-orange colour, using red and yellow paint. This is painted in a stripe on to one end of a long strip of paper. A little more red is added and another strip is painted next to the first one, close enough to allow the two to blur together. The children carry on like this, adding more and more red paint until they reach the other end of the strip, when the paint should be a clear red. Ask visitors to the Senseum when they think the paint stops being orange and starts being red—you'll get as may answers as you get visitors!

These colours can be adapted: red to blue through purple is another possibility, or indeed blue to green. You might like to experiment!

Soundscape

Using a tape machine, record several sounds. Separate each sound with an identification, for example, 'sound A...', 'sound B...', 'sound C...' and so on. Invite your visitors to guess what the sounds are. A good way to do this is to record things 'dropping'. So, for example, sound A might be coins, sound B water, sound C a mug (yes, let it break!)

Tasteurant

Your visitors have to identify different flavours of crisps. Try to choose crisps which look the same—some flavours are different colours. If you want to be very tricky you can use the same flavour but from different manufacturers. Put the crisps in labelled bowls and ask the visitors to write the flavour by the right bowl. If you were being generous you might tell them which flavours you have used, but it is up to you!

Smellorama

Put a variety of items with pungent odours into small, clean pots such as yogurt pots. The game works best when the item is hidden.

The purpose of the Senseum is to demonstrate the variety and complexity of our senses. As a conclusion, place the activity in the context of prayer.

> **Our Father,**
> **You made us, young and old.**
> **You made our senses and you made our world.**
> **You made all the fabulous things that are in it.**
> **We praise you, O God, for everything that you have done,**
> **in the name of Jesus our Lord.**
> **Amen**

Drawing Together

Touching the fingers of God

This act of worship needs some preparation in gathering together the things that remind the group of the patterns of a fingerprint—for example, leaves or the bark of a tree. Take some time in discussion and then decide whether you are going to collect or draw the items. For example, you might think that a butterfly's wing has some of the characteristics of a fingerprint, but it is probably best not to collect these! You may, of course, wish to draw all of the things you think of.

Sit in a circle facing each other.

Reader

O Lord, you live for ever;
long ago you created the earth,
and with your own hands you
made the heavens.

Psalm 102: 24b–25

Each member of the group then stands and says...

We see the hands of God at work throughout our world. His fingers touched the...

. . . .

Insert here the thing that the child has chosen.

After everyone has spoken, say together...

God made our hands with his hands,
our fingers with his fingers.
We reach out to each other and touch
something God made.

All reach out and touch fingertips together, all round the circle.

While still touching, read...

. . . you are always the same,
and your life never ends.

Our children will live in safety,
and under your protection
their descendants will be secure.

Finish with a song if you wish.

Mime

Body music

This is a fascinating activity. Invite the group to use their bodies to make sounds. Slaps and claps are easy, but can anyone make different notes of a scale? Will anyone think of singing as 'body-music'? Remind everyone that we are looking at our uniqueness, not something that anyone can do!

Sounds can be made as a response to the things that God has given in creation.

What would mountain sounds be? Or river sounds? The scope is very great. You could use this activity to just fill in time or you could use it to create a whole 'musical'. The choice is yours.

This activity relates to different world cultures, so you might like to introduce different styles of music from around the world, for example, India, China, Africa, Russia and the Antipodes. You might like to add some animal music, such as dolphin song!

Can you guess where each style of music comes from?

Jesus is coming

Focus

Advent is a important part of the Christian calendar when, as we wait for the coming of the infant king, we are traditionally called to prepare ourselves for the celebration by fasting. The next two sessions take a biblical view of Advent and Christmas, covering the story of Jesus' birth by looking back into the Old Testament after the event of his birth. This is what the gospel writers did. They were not sitting with pad and pencil outside the stable door, waiting to write up the story when Mary and Joseph turned up, like some kind of first-century paparazzi!

This is what Luke told us when we met him on pages 43–47 of *Footsteps and Fingerprints.*

Scene Setter

LUKE 1:26-56

'You will become pregnant and give birth to a son, and you will name him Jesus.'

This is the classic tale of Mary's encounter with Gabriel and her response to the message from God. When reading this passage to (or with) the children, pay special attention to the *Magnificat*—the song of Mary. This will allow you to bring out some of the Old Testament expectations of the Jewish people, of which Mary was, of course, a part.

Discussion Starters

Discuss what it might have been like for Mary, both personally and socially, to receive this message from God.

- ◎ **What might Mary's feelings have been?**
- ★ **What would our feelings have been if we had been Mary?**
- ◎ **How would we expect God to speak to us today?**

Activities

This idea for an Advent calendar is brill. The kind of idea that my dad—who is very old—would call groovy! Ugh!

Advent cubes

You will need three cube nets for each member of the group, like the one illustrated. You may have to make these for the children, but they are not difficult—you just draw around a square template six times and then add the flaps.

Draw the following things on to the cubes. You *must* get the right things on the right cubes, but it doesn't matter which face they go on.

Cube 1: star; angel; hillside; Bethlehem view; road into hills; Jerusalem.

Cube 2: Mary; Mary and Joseph; shepherds and sheep; three kings; Joseph; open stable.

Cube 3: Nazareth; Elizabeth; donkey; night sky; closed stable (outside view); gifts.

We can now make 24 scenes, each with a Bible extract. The scenes and readings run more or less through the 'traditional' story. The children should be able to see clearly that this story is made up of a conflation of the two accounts from Matthew and Luke. The purpose of this Advent calendar is to provide an unusual reading of the story of the coming of Christ. It is not intended to be used in the same way as a conventional calendar, but, modelled on a smaller scale, it could be used as such.

Ensure you draw the scenes before you assemble the cubes!

CUBE 1   CUBE 2   CUBE 3

1. Hillside   Mary   Nazareth

God sent the angel Gabriel to a town called Nazareth. He had a message for a girl.

Luke 1:26–27

2. Angel   Mary   Nazareth

Her name was Mary. The angel came to her and said, 'Peace be with you!'

Luke 1:28

3. Hillside   Joseph   Nazareth

Mary was engaged to Joseph.

Matthew 1:18

4. Angel   Joseph   Nazareth

An angel of the Lord appeared to him and said, 'Joseph, descendant of David, do not be afraid to take Mary as your wife. For it is by the Holy Spirit that she has conceived.'

Matthew 1:20

5. Road   Mary   Elizabeth

Elizabeth said in a loud voice, 'You are the most blessed of all women, and blessed is the child you will bear.'

Luke 1:4–42

6. Hillside   Mary and Joseph   Nazareth

Joseph married Mary as the angel of the Lord had told him to do.

Matthew 1:24

7. Road   Mary and Joseph   Donkey

Emperor Augustus ordered a census. Joseph went from the town of Nazareth. He went with Mary.

Luke 2:1, 4–5

8. Bethlehem   Mary and Joseph   Donkey

Joseph went to the town of Bethlehem with Mary.

Luke 2:4–5

9. Bethlehem   Mary and Joseph   Night sky

While they were in Bethlehem the time came for her to have her baby.

Luke 2:5

10. Bethlehem   Mary and Joseph   Stable

She gave birth to her first son, wrapped him in strips of cloth and laid him in a manger—there was no room for them to stay in the inn.

Luke 2:7

11. Hillside   Shepherds   Night sky

There were some shepherds who were spending the night in the fields, taking care of the sheep...

Luke 2:8

12. Angel   Shepherds   Night sky

An angel of the Lord appeared to them, and the glory of the Lord shone over them. They were terribly afraid, but the angel said to them, 'Don't be afraid! I am here with good news for you, which will bring great joy to all the people. This very day in David's town your Saviour was born—Christ the Lord!'

Luke 2:9–11

13. Angel   Shepherds   Night sky

Suddenly a great army of heaven's angels appeared, singing praises to God: 'Glory to God in the highest heaven, and peace to those with whom he is pleased!'

Luke 2:13–14

14. Bethlehem   Shepherds   Night sky

'Let's go to Bethlehem and see this thing that has happened, which the Lord has told us.'

Luke 2:15

15. Star   Shepherds   Stable

So they hurried off and found Mary and Joseph and saw the baby lying in the manger.

Luke 2:16

16. Star   Mary and Joseph   Stable

Jesus was born in the town of Bethlehem in Judea, during the time when Herod was king.

Matthew 2:1

17. Road   Kings   Gifts

Some men who studied the stars came from the east to Jerusalem.

Matthew 2:1

18. Star   Kings   Night sky

'Where is the baby born to be the king of the Jews? We saw his star when it came up in the east, and we have come to worship him.'

Matthew 2:2

19. Jerusalem   Kings   Night sky

Herod called the visitors from the east to a secret meeting and found out from them the exact time the star had appeared.

Matthew 2:7

20. Bethlehem   Kings   Night sky

He sent them to Bethlehem with these instructions: 'Go and make a careful search for the child.'

Matthew 2:8

21.   Star   Kings   Stable

On their way they saw the same star they had seen in the east. When they saw it, how happy they were, what joy was theirs!

Matthew 2:9-10

22. Bethlehem   Open stable   Night sky

When the shepherds saw him, they told them what the angel had said about the child. All who heard it were amazed at what the shepherds said. Mary remembered these things.

Luke 2:17-18

23. Bethlehem   Open stable   Gifts

When they saw the child with his mother, they knelt down and worshipped him. They brought out their gifts of gold, frankincense and myrrh.

Matthew 2:11

24.   Star   Open stable   Night sky
  (on top of
  other cubes)

She gave birth to her son. And Joseph called him Jesus.

Matthew 1:25

Games

Surprise parcels

> You will need to prepare beforehand by inviting each child to wrap a parcel and bring it to the session.

Elect a team of three or four 'experts' who will have to try to guess what is in the parcels. Everyone else is a 'giver'. If the 'experts' do not guess, then the 'giver' wins a point. If they do guess, then the 'experts' win a point.

To play the game, each of the 'givers' takes it in turn to give a clue as to what is in their parcel. Then each of the 'experts' takes it in turn to guess (they can confer). It is up to you to decide whether the 'experts' are allowed to handle the parcel or only look at it! The idea of the game is for the 'experts' to score more points than the 'givers', whose points are added together.

Drama

The cubes in church

> You will need three large boxes, paper, paint and brushes.

> And some strong people!

You can use the Advent cubes idea for a dramatic presentation in church by drawing the scenes on to large boxes. This can be done by either painting pictures on to paper and then sticking the paper on the boxes, or by painting directly on to the boxes themselves. The first way is safest if you think that you might make mistakes!

The boxes can then be used to present the Christmas story by having the three cubes turned to make the scenes as the short Bible extracts are read out.

Prayers

Lord God,
You have promised many
things in the past, and you have been
faithful to those who love you.
We praise and thank you for the things
we have received and we ask for your
patience as we wait for the things that
you have promised that are yet to
*come. In Jesus' name. **Amen***

Loving Father,
You always have the best things
in mind:
the best for the people who love you,
the best for the world you made.
Help us to be like Mary when you ask
us to work for you, so that what you
intend for the world will happen as it
*should. **Amen***

Drawing Together

Preparing the way

You will need a selection of household objects, such as brushes, cloths and tools to bring forward at the appropriate time.

Start with a song or by playing some music.

All   Prepare a road for the Lord;
              make a straight path for him to travel.

Child 1   I bring a broom, to sweep the Lord's house clean.

Child 2   I bring a hammer to make a chair for the Lord.

Child 3   I bring a pen to write a song of welcome for the Lord.

Child 4   I bring a cloth, to make the Lord's table shine.

Child 5   I bring food to prepare the Lord's feast.

Child 6   I bring a bowl to wash the Lord's tired feet.

All say   Maranatha!
              Come Lord, we are ready.

Close with a prayer.

Mary's song and the angelic announcement of Jesus' birth are not unique in the Bible. The song of Mary bears a striking resemblance to the song of Hannah in 1 Samuel 2:1–10 and you may wish to compare the two with the children. It is a good opportunity to show the continuity of the Bible and the way in which the different parts relate to each other. Another theme that you can use to do this is the theme of 'announced' births. You might like to compare the births of Isaac, Samson, John the Baptist and Jesus.

Theme Extension

The commercialism of Christmas, with all its glitz and glamour, is often blamed for ruining the traditional Christmas. But what we think of as the 'traditional' Christmas is, for the most part, no older than the Victorian era. For example, the service of nine lessons and carols is less than 100 years old and has probably only survived because of the invention of radio!

What we do see, however, is a commercial reappraisal of Christmas which has come about because society is less church-centred than before. The biggest change has probably been in the moving of the celebration forward into Advent. This has meant that Advent is no longer seen as a time of fasting, but it is not to say that the season is any the less Christian. In many ways, piped carols in the shops are no less 'traditional' than Christmas cards or crackers were a century ago, and the important thing to remember is how we as Christians celebrate the coming of our Lord.

If we can give our children a clear picture of what Advent and Christmas mean to them in terms of Christian faith, then they themselves will learn to celebrate it—and maybe in years to come will look back at the Christmases of their childhood with nostalgic yearning! Whatever we think of the commercialism, this is the world in which our children live and many of them find it exciting and exhilarating. Exploring the traditions of Christmas would be an excellent way to extend the theme and help the children to understand why we do certain things at Christmas.

Elizabeth and Zechariah

Focus

This session aims to develop an awareness that God sometimes acts in unexpected ways which we might find hard to believe. We have to learn to trust him.

We met Elizabeth in the temple in Jerusalem on pages 22–28 of **Footsteps and Fingerprints**.

Scene Setter

There is a sense of 'expect the unexpected' in the angel's message to Zechariah regarding the birth of John. But should we assume that Zechariah *was* expecting the unexpected? It is easy with the wisdom of hindsight to wonder why Zechariah didn't believe the angel's message. We might feel that, as a priest serving the God of miracles, it would have been more natural for him to have believed the angel. But, as Zechariah himself reasoned, he was an old man and his wife, Elizabeth, was also old. How often have we felt more at home with reason than with the unexplained mystery of the miraculous? This story serves to remind us, in an almost comical way, that our God is a God of miracles. Should not we, too, learn to expect him to act in a miraculous way?

LUKE 1:5–25 AND 57–80

Zechariah said to the angel, 'How shall I know if this is so? I am an old man, and my wife is old also.'

Prepare for the session by reading the whole of the story of Zechariah and Elizabeth, and then, once you are sure of the order of events, use the following points as a frame to retell the story to your group.

★ Zechariah and Elizabeth were an elderly couple with no children, but they dedicated their lives to God.

☉ One day, while Zechariah was in the temple, an angel appeared to him and told him that Elizabeth was going to have a baby.

★ Zechariah didn't believe the angel—both he and Elizabeth were much too old to start a family!

☉ The angel insisted that what he said was true and caused Zechariah to be struck dumb until the baby was born, as a sign that his message would indeed come true.

★ Zechariah was unable to speak right up to the time when his son was born.

☉ In fact, he had to write the baby's name down so that people would know that he was to be called 'John'.

★ As soon as he did this, he found his voice again and sang a song of praise to God.

Discussion Starters

You might like to prepare for this discussion by collecting together some pictures of angels—there are many depictions of angels, both in classic and contemporary art—and looking up some of the Bible references where angels appear.

☉ **Do you believe in angels?**

★ **What do you think an angel looks like?**

☉ **How would you respond if an angel spoke to you?**

★ **Do you know any other stories in the Bible about angels appearing to people?**

☉ **Who did the angel appear to and why?**

Activities
Sharing in the joy of the birth of a child

You'll need sheets of plain paper, paints and brushes.

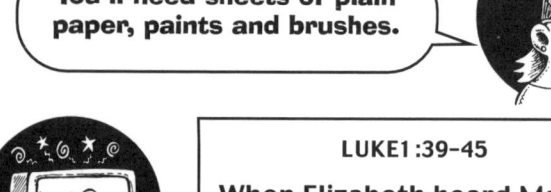

LUKE1:39–45

When Elizabeth heard Mary's greeting, the baby moved within her.

Read aloud the words of Elizabeth to Mary:

'You are the most blessed of all women, and blessed is the child you will bear! Why should this great thing happen to me, that my Lord's mother comes to visit me? For as soon as I heard your greeting, the baby within me jumped with gladness. How happy you are to believe that the Lord's message to you will come true!'

The overwhelming joy of Elizabeth's response is justly famous. This tremendous scene lends itself well to being expressed through art. Encourage your group to think of the joy expressed: joyous faces, joyous movements, joyous colours and patterns. What colours would they use to show joy? What shapes? Older members of the group might like to try to paint the joy of the unborn baby as he leaps inside his mother.

The following poem is full of lively, evocative images which tumble from the poet's pen in a profuse jumble of joy. Not all the images are immediately understandable, but this doesn't seem to matter; it is primarily a song of unexpected joy for the childhood yet to begin.

You're

Clownlike, happiest on your hands,
Feet to the stars, and moon-skulled,
Gilled like a fish. A common-sense
Thumbs down on the Dodo's mode.
Wrapped up in yourself like a spool,
Trawling your dark as owls do.
Mute as a turnip from the Fourth
Of July to All Fools' Day,
O high-riser, my little loaf.

Vague as fog and looked for like mail.
Farther off than Australia.
Bent-backed Atlas, our travelled prawn.
Snug as a bud and at home
Like a sprat in a pickle jug
A creel of eels, all ripples.
Jumpy as a Mexican bean.
Right, like a well done sum.
A clean slate, with your own face on.

Sylvia Plath

Expression in silence—creating images of emotion

Zechariah's song of praise to God when John is born is an expression of joy, flooding out in a tumble of images.

LUKE 1:68–79

Read Zechariah's prophetic song aloud.

What images, colours or shapes does Zechariah's song conjure up?

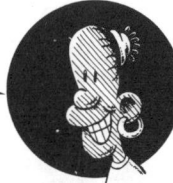

Here are some suggestions to help you...

	Image	Colour	Shape
Let us praise the Lord	trumpet	gold/yellow	circle
The God of Israel	clouds	purple	diamond
He has come to the help	hand	blue/white	cross
of his people	broken	red/black	jagged
and has set them free	chain	grey	square

You may only want to use a few verses, rather than the whole prophecy.

The responses to this exercise may range from very tentative experimentation to bold expression. Do not be surprised if some of the images portray violence; freedom has a violent history in our world, not least in the crucifixion. If you are familiar with Latin American (liberation) religious art, you may know of some pictures which the children would find helpful and interesting as expressions of Christ's death and resurrection.

Games

Charades—a silent game

Split the group into teams of three or four and give each team part of the story of Zechariah and Elizabeth. Each team has to work out a mime to perform to the rest of the group, who have then to decide which part of the story is being depicted.

Sketchwords

You'll need sheets of plain paper and pencils for this game.

Choose a selection of words from the story of Zechariah and Elizabeth—you'll need a list of about fifteen altogether. Split the group into teams of four or five. Number the team members. The first player in each team comes to the leader who whispers a word, for example 'angel'. The players then run back to their team and, in silence, draw the word. When the rest of the team have guessed correctly (they have to do this quietly to prevent the other teams overhearing), the next player runs to the leader and whispers the word to them. If they are right they are given a fresh word. The first team to guess each word is the winner.

The words could include...
Herod, priest, temple, altar, crowd, angel, children, message, hands, town, hills, house, baby, joy, writing-tablet, road, dawn, steps...

Mime or Dance

You might like to use mime or dance to express the reactions of people to the events in the story. For example:

⊚ How does Zechariah respond to the angel?

★ How does the crowd respond to Zechariah?

⊚ How does Elizabeth respond when she realizes she is going to have a baby?

★ How does Elizabeth respond to Mary?

⊚ How does Zechariah respond to God when John is born?

Split into smaller teams of three or four to think about the responses and work out how to express them in mime or dance. The work needs to express the *emotions* being conveyed, not just the event itself.

Prayers

Father God,
It is very easy for us to
miss the signs of your presence
in our daily lives,
and easy to forget that you are the God
of miracles.
Help us never to forget that your
miracle of creation surrounds us.
Help us to look for your miracles in your
word, our Bible,
and in our lives. Amen

Almighty God,
Thank you for the people who heard
your voice
and did as you asked.
Thank you that through them we can
learn about you.
Help us, too, to do as you ask:
in telling others about you;
in being a friend to those who
are lonely;
in bringing joy to those who are sad;
in caring for your world. Amen

Theme Extension

If you are able to visit a selection of churches in your local area you might like to see how different churches express something about God in the way they are built and from their interior design. Their design is a silent expression of the presence of God. Look for what the church is saying about God through its windows, its shape, the way that colour and light are used, its decorations (or lack of them). If the church you visit is old, how would its design have helped people to worship God in the days before everyone could read?

Calendar Link

This session is a introduction to Advent. You can delve deeper into the Lectionary link by exploring the rich mixture of Old and New Testament expectation that are highlighted at this time.

Drawing Together

Silent worship

Ask the children to sit in groups of about four. Give each group a short song, or a short prayer, and ask them to express its meaning with their hands (rather like sign language).

After a few minutes ask each group to share their prayer or song with everyone. This is done in silence, with each group taking turns to contribute.

End with a short silence. If you are able to sign a prayer, you might like to sign the prayer in silence together.

Jesus is born

Focus

In Matthew's gospel the birth of Jesus bursts upon us in good, solid Old Testament style, complete with the (often ignored) addition of a carefully arranged genealogy. We might not be too familiar with the genealogy, but, in many ways, the stories of Jesus' birth are too well known—and sometimes familiarity breeds contempt. Many children have heard the nativity story year in and year out and will need to be presented with a fresh approach in order to understand the story with new eyes and see afresh the birth of our Lord.

> We missed the birth of Jesus, we were too busy hiding from the soldiers.

> Yeah, that was in Footsteps and... er...

> Fingerprints. Pages 59–64. If I wasn't here...

> **MATTHEW 1:1—2:12 AND LUKE 2:1–20**
>
> **Matthew 1:18: This is how the birth of Jesus Christ took place...**

Scene Setter

The two stories are similar in their approach, although quite different in their content. The main points can be summarized as follows:

The genealogy of Jesus—establishing Jesus' legitimate kingship

Matthew 1:1–17
Jesus' ancestors are listed in true Jewish style, only giving the important people in the family tree. Jesus is shown to have descended from Abraham through David. Not only is he thus established as a Jew in the fullest sense, he is also from the kingly line.

The miraculous conception and the angel's visit to Joseph

Matthew 1:18–24
Joseph is distressed at the news of Mary's pregnancy. He is dissuaded from divorcing her by the angel.

The journey to Bethlehem

Luke 2:1–4
The need for the journey was created by the Roman emperor. Little is known about the journey, it probably was rather uncomfortable for Mary but we are not told that. And there is no record of a donkey either!

The birth

Luke 2:5–7
Jesus is born and laid in the manger—there is no room for them to stay in the inn.

The shepherds and the angels

Luke 2:8–20
The shepherds are told directly of the birth of God's son by the messengers of God. They arrive mystified and go back to their flocks rejoicing.

The visit of the magi

Matthew 2:1–12
Jesus is recorded by Matthew as being in a house, where the magi find him. They have come because they have read the natural signs of the world correctly. Scholars, wise in the interpretation of the ancient scriptures, direct them to Bethlehem and again Jesus is shown to be fulfilling the ancient prophecies.

Discussion Starters

Don't add any traditional details; for example, encourage the children to notice for themselves that there is no mention of a stable.

★ **What's missing from each story?**

☺ **Why are there two stories?**

★ **Which story do you like best?**

☺ **Why?**

Activities

A nativity sculpture

You will need a selection of card rolls, ping-pong or polystyrene balls, scraps of fabric, card, glue, crayons and scissors.

The design of a nativity scene says a great deal about where and by whom it was made. If possible it would be helpful to have a selection from different parts of the world, made from different materials. For example, some express the joy of the birth, some the lowliness of the birth, some the kingship of Jesus, some Jesus' links with heaven and some his links with earth. If you don't have access to actual nativity scenes, invite the children to discuss what they themselves have seen.

This activity encourages the group to express their own thoughts about Jesus. For example, they might think of him primarily as a storyteller, or a healer, or a friend. The kings brought gifts of gold, frankincense and myrrh. Encourage the children to include themselves in their nativity scene, bringing gifts which appropriately express their own feelings.

Before you begin, discuss together what kind of nativity everyone wants to make. Is it to be a 'Luke' nativity with shepherds and a manger, or a 'Matthew' nativity with kings and a house? Or is it to be a traditional mixture of the two?

Once everyone has decided, each child needs to make all the component parts of their nativity scene. Figures can be made with cardboard rolls (from clingfilm or foil rolls) topped with ping-pong or polystyrene balls, or dolly pegs with the legs sawn off so they stand up easily. Each figure can then be dressed with scraps of fabric, and cardboard arms added if desired. Animals and gifts can be made from card and coloured in. Once the figures are made they can be set out on a backdrop of card to show the setting of the nativity scene.

The art of the birth of Jesus

You'll need a selection of pictures depicting the nativity. You can find these in a variety of books and magazines about art.

We found some really good ones in our local library.

It is not always easy for children to understand the intention of the artist in a classical painting. This activity aims to encourage them, not only to see the birth of Jesus through new eyes, but also to learn a little about classical art!

Throughout history, artistic interpretation of Jesus' birth has tended to be less eclectic and rather closer to the biblical texts than our devotional nativity scenes are today. Whilst we might find the forms and fashions of classical art difficult, the artists are usually meticulous about the detail they include. For example, with the visitors from the east, the scene is often depicted using very expensive materials such as gold leaf. Blue paint made of lapis lazuli (mixed with egg yolk or oil) was also used because it was expensive and showed the glory and riches of the newborn king, or the inestimable value of Mary, with her traditionally blue robe painted with lapis lazuli. It also showed, of course, the importance of the person paying for the painting!

Take some time discussing a selection of classic paintings and noting some of the things that they are trying to represent, and then invite the children to create their own pictures. Encourage the group to draw out the meaning of the birth of Christ in their picture, rather than just painting the scene. For example:

★ **Use rustic browns and greens to show Jesus' humble birth.**

⊚ **Use bright colours and happy faces to express joy.**

★ **Use pieces of gold cloth or foil to emphasize the richness of the king.**

> This activity could be set up with different tables for each interpretation, each with the appropriate materials on it for the children to use for their pictures.

Announced births in the Bible

This activity could be extended to explore the early church's understanding of who Jesus was. In the same way that we see images and colours in art, we see the beginning of Christian understanding in the Bible, and the birth of Jesus gives us an opportunity to look closely at the Bible and see what it is that the gospel writers thought about Jesus' birth. Older children can begin to explore some of the Old Testament references in the Christmas story. These can be found in the footnotes in most Bibles and there is great value in looking up the references rather than just being told about them. For example:

⊚ **Matthew 1:23 and Isaiah 7:14: The gospel writer tells us that we can now see Jesus as the fulfilment of Isaiah's prophecy.**

★ **Matthew 2:6 is taken from Micah 5:2.**

The Virgin by Adrian Snell tells the Christmas story very effectively and, in fact, provides an accessible way to touch on the slaughter of the innocents. The original version (Pilgrim Records, Marshall, Morgan & Scott, 1981), is more musically arresting than his later version and would probably capture the imagination rather more easily. *The Virgin* has a striking set of prophecies in its opening sequences. Equally, you could pick out the relevant sections of Handel's *Messiah*, which gives a wealth of biblical material concerning Christ's birth.

Games

Who am I?

Introduce the game by pointing out that the shepherds and wise men knew who Jesus was, but Herod's advisers were less sure. Sit the group in a circle and invite everyone to choose a famous character from TV, history, stage or screen. Each child takes a turn to give a clue to who their character is, and the rest of the group has to try to guess their identity. The person giving the clue may only answer 'yes' or 'no' to the question. Allow only one guess to each clue as you go round the circle. You might need to limit the overall number of guesses to ten or twenty. Anyone not out at that point wins the game and reveals their identity.

Prayers
Heavenly Father,
We come before you as
your children.
No matter what our age,
you care for us and keep us safe.
Through your word,
help us to see the example of your son
Jesus clearly,
so that we may follow him
truly. Amen

Almighty God,
We marvel at the miracle
of your coming to us as a
tiny baby.
We marvel at the miracle of your love
for us despite our failings.
We marvel at the miracle of your
presence with us today.
In the gift of your son, Jesus,
in the gift of your Holy Spirit,
we marvel at the love so freely given,
so undeserved.
Lord God, thank you for miracles. **Amen**

Dear Father,
Amid all the rush and excitement
of Christmas,
the lights, the music and the laughter,
help us to remember that there are
many who suffer, who are sad and
alone.
Help us to remember how desperately
they need your love.
Be with all who long for you this
Christmas, we pray. **Amen**

Reader 1	What do you bring to the baby king?
Child	We bring gifts from Luke
Child	The people's gifts, the work of our hands
Child	Cloth—from wool, cared for by shepherds
Child	Paper—from trees
Child	A key—from the earth
Reader 1	What do you bring to the baby king?
Child	We bring gifts from Matthew
Child	Gifts from our wealth
Child	Gifts of gold
Child	Gifts of perfume
Child	Gifts of precious ointment
Reader 1	What do you bring to the baby king?
Child	We bring gifts from John
Child	The gifts that Christ brought with him
Child	The gift of light
Child	And the gift of love

You can sing a carol or two if you wish, but you might prefer to keep the act of worship very short and simple.

Drawing Together

What shall we bring to the baby?

You'll need a selection of items to represent the gifts being brought. These can be actual items, pictures or drawings.

In this act of worship we offer our own gifts to God, and thankfully receive gifts from him.

Choose one person to ask the questions, then invite others to step forward and present the items. In the final section, 'gifts from John', the children bring a Bible.

Calendar Link

The links with Christmas and Epiphany are fairly obvious. The church calendar tends to focus on specific and important aspects of Jesus' birth and it can often be confusing to try and work out what is happening in the 'gaps'. What were Jesus' family doing between his birth and the arrival of the magi, for example, or did the magi arrive at the same time as the shepherds? Discuss with the group the things that must have gone on around the main events such as cooking, working, travelling and resting.

The church calendar might give younger children the impression that Jesus died five months after his birth, and care is therefore needed to explain the time spans between each event.

Spring
TERM

God calls Moses

Focus

Moses holds a unique place in the Old Testament and thus in the Bible as a whole—and, of course, throughout Christianity. He was the great leader who took the Israelites out of Egypt. That is how he is remembered in later history (Psalm 105:26–27; Malachi 4:4). The book of Exodus doesn't paint a very favourable picture of Moses to start with, as we see him disagreeing with God and not doing as he is asked until God agrees to send Aaron with him! There is a great deal of simple humanity in these exchanges (Exodus chapters 3 and 4), with which we can feel an affinity.

> Moses was happier to play football than to do as God asked when we met him on pages 4–9 of Friends and Followers!

Scene Setter

The Burning Bush

> EXODUS 3 AND 4
>
> There the angel of the Lord appeared to him as a flame coming from the middle of a bush.

Here is an opportunity to explore what it means to 'have a calling'. We tend to think of 'a calling' as being something, a little like conversion, which produces a sudden change in the direction of our lives. This is clearly true in Moses' case, but he does not accept his calling with ease. To what extent can his response be seen as a matter of disobedience rather than questioning the call? When we think of what it means to have a calling nowadays, we are not usually thinking of the kind of work that Moses was called to do—so how was Moses' calling different?

You might like to briefly outline the story of Moses as he runs away from Egypt.

@ **Moses goes to see his fellow Hebrews. (Exodus 2:11)**

@ **Moses is horrified at the treatment of the Hebrews and kills a soldier. (Exodus 2:12)**

@ **Moses returns, but is identified as the killer by the Hebrews. (Exodus 2:14)**

@ **In fear, Moses runs away to Midian where he has to earn a living shepherding Jethro's sheep and goats. (Exodus 2:15–21)**

Discussion Starters

⊚ Why was Moses out in the desert in the first place?

★ Why did he remove his shoes?

⊚ What is so important about being barefoot? We might think that taking shoes off is *less* respectful to those around, including God.

★ Who made the shoes we wear? Who made our feet?

Activities

> You will need card, coloured cellophane (some sweet wrappers are ideal), glue, sellotape, safety scissors, pencils, crayons/felt-tip pens, coloured paper, small blocks of wood (off-cuts from a DIY shop or wood yard) and a small battery-powered lamp or torch.

> If you are ambitious you might also like to collect together bulbs, bulb holders, batteries and wire.

Stained-glass bushes

There are two ways to make stained-glass bushes. The simplest is to trace the illustration below on to card and colour it in. Cut out the flame shapes around its branches and glue the cellophane behind them to represent the flames.

Fold the card or attach the bottom of the bush to a wooden block, then set up a light to shine through from behind, thus illuminating the flames. Do not use a candle.

Alternatively, you could bend the card into a cylinder shape and place a torch bulb inside, connected to a battery.

Hearing God's call

This activity needs paper, glue, scissors, a selection of mail order catalogues and magazines, pens and pencils.

This activity links in with the worship suggestion in this section.

Start the activity by discussing ways in which we might hear God speak to us today. Explore how God speaks through the Bible, through the church, or perhaps through different things that happen to us in life.

Follow this with a look at what a prophet is. What does prophecy mean to the members of your group? Is a prophet someone who speaks about the future, like some kind of holy horoscope? Go on to show how the prophets, whilst speaking of the future, were primarily concerned with *speaking out* the words of God.

God called Moses when he was least expecting it. Explore with the children unexpected ways that God might speak to us, for example:

⊚ **through a television programme**

⊚ **through a news bulletin**

⊚ **through pop music**

⊚ **through a charity event such as Red Nose Day**

Distribute the catalogues around the group and invite them to cut out pictures that suggest something that God is saying to them. For example, training shoes might speak to us about the need to do something for those who live in poverty.

Build their ideas into a collage and write a few words about what God might be saying through each idea.

Games

Leading and following—sometimes you have to do both

Moses followed God, but he also led the people of Israel. A blindfold game is a fun way to illustrate this. Set up a simple route around the room, under tables, through things, etc. If you have access to PE benches, these could be used as well. Don't use professional PE apparatus.

Split your group into teams of five or six. Each team chooses one person *not* to be blindfolded, the others wear blindfolds. Each team stands in a line, holding hands with the unblindfolded person at the head of the line. The unblindfolded person then has to lead the others around the route by whispering instructions to the person next in line.

Turn right...

The instructions then have to be passed from person to person by whispering along the line of blindfolded people. No one is to pull another team member around the course, they have to feel their way based on the instructions they are given. The members of the teams will then find themselves in Moses' position. They are following a leader but are also having to lead others.

This activity is a good team-building exercise. If anyone feels uncomfortable about being blindfolded, be encouraging, but don't force them to join in.

What's in a name?

One of the most important parts of the story of God's calling of Moses is the revelation of the divine name YAHWEH (I AM).

EXODUS 3:13–15.

This name is considered so holy that Jewish people will not speak it. Christianity has no such scruples and has several forms of the name of God.

The significance of names is a well-known facet of human society, and it seems always to have been so. Knowing God's name doesn't give Moses power over God, but it does give him authority, particularly as it is associated with God's 'credentials': 'Tell the Israelites that I, the Lord, the God of their ancestors, the God of Abraham, Isaac, and Jacob, have sent you...'

You'll need a selection of books which give the meaning of names.

Split the group into teams of three or four and give each team a list of about ten names—a different list for each team. Ask them to find the correct meaning of each name on the list and then make up two other false meanings. When they have done this, each team takes it in turn to read the three meanings of one of the names on their list. The other team(s) have to guess which meaning is the correct one. If the guess is correct, the team who guessed scores a point; if it is incorrect, the team who gave the meaning scores a point. Keep a tally of the score. The winning team is the one with the most points at the end of the game.

You might like to go on to explore the importance of names to the group. Why are we given names? Do they know what their names mean?

Prayers

Father God,
You are the one who led
the family of Abraham
out of the land of Egypt.
You worked in Moses, an ordinary man.
Be with us, ordinary people,
and give us the strength
to work for you as Moses did. **Amen**

Dear Lord,
You work in your people throughout
the world.
Each of us is different and
each of us is called to a different task.
Help us to hear when you call us and
give us the strength to do our task—
just as you did with Moses. **Amen**

Mighty God,
Through Moses you changed the lives
of many people.
Help us to hear your call
so that through us
lives around your world
will continue to be changed. **Amen**

Drawing Together

Ask the group to sit in a circle, holding their stained-glass bushes. Open with a prayer.

Leader

Moses met God through the miracle of the burning bush.

Everyone places their stained-glass bush in the middle of the circle.

Leader

He took off his shoes because he was on holy ground.

Everyone removes their shoes and puts them behind them (outside the circle).

All

We meet God through the things that happen in our lives, just as Moses did. And we meet him through his holy word, the Bible.

Leader

Moses said to God, 'I am nobody. How can I go to the king and bring the Israelites out of Egypt?'

All

God answered, 'I will be with you, and when you bring the people out of Egypt, you will worship me on this mountain. That will be proof that I have sent you.'

Everyone puts their shoes back on, stands up and holds hands around the circle.

Leader

God said to Moses, 'I will help you to speak, and I will tell you what to say.'

The leader places the Bible in the middle of the circle.

End with a song and say the Grace together.

Theme Extension

This extension provides an opportunity to explore 'calling' in more personal terms. Arrange for your minister to talk to the group about their 'calling'. You could arrange for a series of such visitors. People experience their calling in very different ways and have as many different ways of talking about it. Their testimony may be an inspiration to members of your group, who might already have had thoughts about what they want to do when they grow up. This is a good opportunity to enable them to learn how others have listened to God and done what he asked them to do.

Teamwork

Focus

The major part of this session is based on working together, and each activity is designed to explore the implications of working as a team. Although some of the activities might seem light-hearted, there is a serious side in that the members of the team will need to explore the dynamics of the team in order for everything to run smoothly. As their leader, you'll need to be prepared to step in when things are not quite developing to plan!

We usually work as a team, but just occasionally, like in Friends and Followers, pages 39–44, we kinda get it wrong.

Scene Setter

The feeding of the 5000

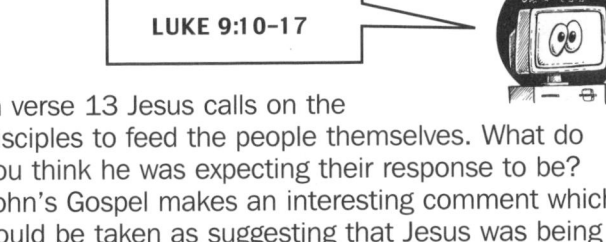

LUKE 9:10-17

In verse 13 Jesus calls on the disciples to feed the people themselves. What do you think he was expecting their response to be? John's Gospel makes an interesting comment which could be taken as suggesting that Jesus was being deliberately provocative (John 6:6). If the disciples had provided the food, then the miracle would not have taken place, but we sense that Jesus knew they were unable to provide for the people by themselves. It is striking to note, however, that Jesus performs the miracle in collaboration with God (v. 16: 'Jesus took the five loaves and two fish, looked up to heaven, thanked God for them, broke them, and gave them to the people').
The miracle becomes a lesson in our dependence on God in the provision of our daily needs.

Discussion Starters

When we are alone we can sometimes feel so weak and tired that we cannot seem to achieve anything.

★ **What tasks can we think of that we simply cannot do alone?**

★ **Does it matter who we do things with?**

★ **Do some people make us feel stronger than others?**

★ **What about parents, friends, teachers or other people in the church?**

★ **Which people in our communities work as teams? Sales teams, rescue teams, sports teams…**

MATTHEW 18:19-20

'And I tell you…: whenever two of you on earth agree about anything you pray for, it will be done for you by my Father in heaven. For where two or three come together in my name, I am there with them.'

Explain to the children that these words of Jesus are a very significant comment about the value of teamwork and communicating. The focus is on prayer. Many of our prayers are of the 'letter to Santa' variety. What Jesus is saying is that prayer is something that we do together, as a community, praying is not just something individuals do in private. Of course we do pray on our own, but, in a sense, when we pray we are joining a stream of prayer that is being constantly created by the people of God.

Think for a moment about the various purposes of prayer, for example:

⊚ **Adoration**

⊚ **Confession**

⊚ **Praise**

⊚ **Supplication**

⊚ **Thanksgiving**

⊚ **Forgiveness**

Go on to invite your group to write prayers of their own and then share them with the whole group. Be sensitive if the prayers have a personal content; this is after all what prayer is for!

Explain that the word 'Amen' is used to show that we all agree with the person's prayer.

Games

Tug of war, if you must!

Choose teams carefully. It is possible for younger people to hurt themselves if their teams are unbalanced. You will need a good thick rope, preferably not a nylon one.

Fill the bucket!

You need a large container full of water, lots of sponges and some buckets.

This game must be played out of doors—preferably on a warm day so that everyone can dry off afterwards.

Mark out the area where the game is to be played as illustrated. You might like to ask everyone to bring wellies and plastic aprons for protection!

Or swimming costumes!

The object of the game is to get water from the container to the buckets using the sponges. You can throw them, carry them or use any other means you can think of. The game may end in one of three ways:

1. **A bucket is actually filled. (This is almost impossible!)**

2. **A pre-set time limit is reached (say, four minutes).**

3. **The container is emptied.**

In the case of the last two you will have to have a judge to measure the water and see who has collected the most.

More traditional team games would also fit nicely into this theme. You could arrange to play football at a local park, or have a sports day where you have all sorts of different kinds of relay games. The ones where children have to crawl under each other's legs always go down well!

If you have problems with grounds or weather, you could arrange a swimming gala at a local pool. These can often be hired for private functions. Make sure that you have adequate supervision and get some help from a swimming teacher about different races etc. Galas are based on teamwork—so everyone will have to do their best.

A teamwork presentation

First of all, set the following scenario:

Once upon a time there was a group of friends who wanted to buy something which they could all play with together. Everyone made a suggestion: a go-kart, a basketball and a kite were just three things they thought of—you might be able to think of others. They decided to start saving some money together, so they all went out and did jobs for a whole week. They needed ten pounds and, at the end of the week, they sat down and put their money in the middle of the group. They had collected exactly nine pounds. Then somebody noticed that one of them had not put anything in the middle and said...

At this point invite the children to take up the story. If you have a large group divide them into smaller teams of four or five. They must plan the rest of the story as a play that can be performed to the rest of the group. They need to bear in mind that there may be several reasons why one person did not contribute their money. The play must end with the object being bought.

Activities

Preparing a feast

This would be an especially good activity for the patronal festival of a church, when everyone can join in the party. You might need to ask for some extra help with the preparation, but the children should be encouraged to do as much as they can for themselves.

Start by discussing the following with the group:

- What will the menu be?
- ★ How will the food be presented?
- Who will be given which task?

> You might like to use collage for your mats, or make them out of cloth using dye pens to decorate them.

The menu

Food such as sausages on sticks, simple sandwiches or pasta salads can be brought from home. Make sure that the suggestions are all easy to prepare.

> My Pinwheel Surprises are easy to make in a short time. You'll find the recipe on page 10 of Families and Feelings.

> We made cracker faces for our party. These are great fun—spread cream cheese on to a cream cracker and then make a face with bits of tomato, cucumber, peppers, carrot, anything really. You can even use parsley to make hair!

Place mats

Before preparing the food, invite each child to make a place mat to be used at the table.

> You'll need a sheet of A4 paper for each child, pencils, crayons, felt-tip pens or paint, and clear plastic film.

Follow the theme by suggesting examples of teamwork such as games, preparing meals, fire crews, ambulance or ship's crew as illustrations for the mats. When the mats are finished they can be covered in clear plastic film. Alternatively, you may wish to have them laminated by a local business supplier or printshop. When they are laminated they will look much brighter and will be wipe-clean so they can be used many times. They will *not*, however, be properly heat-resistant and this needs pointing out to the children.

> Mine had chocolate spread and pieces of crystallized fruit and small sweets—they were scrummy!

To present the food it is a good idea to use paper plates, but don't decorate them—nobody wants to eat felt pen!

Once the food has been prepared, everyone needs to be assigned a role in order for the food to be set out, served and everything cleared away afterwards. Those who are to be waiters might want to dress up—this could be everyone if parents and other members of the church are to be invited to the party. The whole thing is intended to be fun and colourful.

Prayers

Dear Father,
When we work together,
things can be great fun,
but when we argue and row, things get
spoiled—sometimes they get broken
and can never be mended.
Be with each of us and help us to work
together so that nothing will be spoiled
and we can all praise you as we should.
Amen

Lord,
There are many people who do not get
on together;
this has brought war and sadness
across the whole world.
We pray for your world, that wars will
end
and that everyone will be given the
chance to work for peace.
In Jesus' name. Amen

Drawing Together

Invite parents and others to come to a meal. The children will be serving the food and drinks to their guests.

When everyone has arrived, welcome them by explaining that you are learning how to work together, and open with a prayer. Once the food is served, use a grace before eating and, finally, close the meal with a prayer of thanks.

A grace

Father of us all,
We praise you for this food and
for all those who contributed to
our having it.
For the people who grew it,
for the people who harvested it
and for the people who prepared it.
We praise you for this food. Amen

The city of peace Jerusalem

Focus

This session focuses first on the nation of Israel and the Jerusalem-centred worldview of the Old Testament. It then moves into the current state of modern-day Jerusalem. This is vitally important as we encounter the present day Arab/Israeli strife in our news bulletins.

The session then moves beyond the present day to the Jerusalem which is the new city of God in the book of Revelation (21:9ff).

We've been to Jerusalem many times in our adventures. We learned about its history from David in Tiptoes and Fingertips. You'll find the story on pages 11–16.

Scene Setter

ZECHARIAH 8:1–5

'I have longed to help Jerusalem because of my deep love for her people...'

This is a lovely vision of the new Jerusalem, an idyllic place, but anchored in the real human world. We would like all our towns to look like this. Look at holiday snaps of town squares and discuss what people are doing—this is just how Zechariah describes it, with everyone peacefully going about their everyday business.

REVELATION 21:10—22:3

This reading is like a dream sequence. Read Revelation 21:16–27 to the children. Can they imagine a city like this? In what ways is it similar to Zechariah's description of Jerusalem? Does it capture the same desire for security and calm?

Discussion Starters

Start by discussing what it is that makes somewhere important. Ask the children to identify places that are important to them, for example, school, church, friend's house, dad's house, gran's house.

Go on to read Revelation 22:1–2. What are all the different things in the New Jerusalem for?

- the precious stones?
- the river?
- the tree?

Discuss older maps and their convention of putting Jerusalem at the centre, because it is God's city, a holy city. These maps are, of course, from our western society, and indeed many of them were drawn while Jerusalem was under Muslim control—perhaps they were a kind of wishful thinking...

Here is an opportunity for children to do some wishful thinking of their own.

It could be said that Zechariah was being wishful when he gave his prophecy about the new Jerusalem, but perhaps not.

Ask the children to look up some other passages about Jerusalem; try these:

2 CHRONICLES 6:5–6

Solomon speaks the words of God to David, and God specifically names Jerusalem as the place where the temple is to be built.

PSALM 51:18

A good example of the description of Jerusalem as Zion. It is a common feature of Hebrew poetry to repeat the first half of a verse in the second half, but using different words. In this verse, Zion is in the first half and Jerusalem in the second.

ISAIAH 65:18

These Old Testament words indicate that Jerusalem is God's 'chosen' city.

Children enjoy making discoveries and might well enjoy using a concordance to find all the references to Jerusalem that they can. The group should be able to use indexes reasonably well. If you do this, get them to put the things they find into two sets, one about the actual city of Jerusalem and one where Jerusalem is being described as the heavenly city of God.

Another way to approach this would be to make it a game in which the players have to collect cards with references on them, and then look them up in their Bibles. Whoever finds the reference first, and then works out whether it is about the earthly Jerusalem or the new Jerusalem, is the winner.

The children can then look up some of the New Testament references to Jerusalem. This in particular gives an opportunity to look forward into the Christian hope.

Activities

Map-making

Imitating the art of medieval map-making, make your own maps of the world. Each child can do this in one of two ways.

1. **By putting the place which is most important to them in the centre, and then putting other things around it.**

2. **By putting themselves at the centre and arranging other things which touch their lives around the picture of themselves.**

Point out that the ancient map-makers put all sorts of things into their maps that came from stories and ancient myths, as well as the things that they may have seen on their own travels. So, include on the maps places where animals from fiction live, places where strange plants grow, places where dreams are made and so on.

It might have been a dream landscape that C.S. Lewis had in mind when he wrote *The Last Battle* and gave us a picture of Aslan's country: 'That country and this country—all the *real* countries—are only spurs jutting out from the great mountains of Aslan...' (C.S. Lewis, *The Last Battle*, chapter 16). Children could be encouraged to read the Chronicles of Narnia. Some of the ideas are rather dated now, but once children 'get the bug', they won't be able to put them down!

The New Jerusalem— a colourful collage

You'll need a large piece of paper, a selection of fabrics and different materials, glue and scissors.

The city can be drawn out on a large piece of paper, and different fabrics and materials stuck on to represent the different precious stones and the different things in the city—the river, the tree of life, and the walls, for example.

It would be good to include the scene from Zechariah somewhere in the city.

If you have the right materials you could make this into a banner to hang in church. Banners need not be over-complex and can be glued together very easily with Copydex or similar child-friendly glues. However, beware of including too many tiny details as these will not stick well.

Prayers

Our Father,
We thank you for places
which are special to you:
for Jerusalem, your holy city;
for our churches, your houses;
for our hearts where we can invite you
into our lives. Amen

Dear Lord,
When we look at the cities of our world
we do not see peace,
but sadness and violence.
Help all those who are sad or lost
or victims of unrest,
and help us to make our cities more
like the new Jerusalem that is to come.
Amen

Almighty God,
We pray for your city, Jerusalem,
for all those who live there,
of whatever faith, or none—
Muslim, Jew and Christian.
May they all recognize your peace
and live in your love,
working together to end the strife
between them.
In Jesus' name. Amen

Drawing Together

If your church has missionary links, they could form part of this act of worship.

This act of worship requires you to make a tree! Not a real one, a large drawing will do. Attach as many cut-out leaves to the tree as there are children in your group. You will also need a large map of the world pinned up on a wall or board.

Reader   Revelation 22:1–3
Leader 1

Sit quietly and think of people around the world we live in. In many ways it is a world full of poverty, war, sadness, distress, and loneliness.

Show some pictures or even a video of some news clips to illustrate this.

Now think of one of these places or groups of people to pray for.

Leader 2

Collect a leaf from the tree. Imagine that you have taken the leaf from the tree of peace.

Pray for peace, for the place you are thinking of.

Pause for prayer.

Stick your leaf in the right place on the map.

Have an adult by the map with some Blu-tack. They can also help to locate the places.

Close with a song.

Theme Extension

'Jerusalem' means 'city of peace'. Do you know what the names of the towns in your area mean?

Many English towns have very old names. Towns with names ending in 'wick', 'thorpe' or 'ham' are quite common: Berwick and Scunthorpe, for instance. 'Wick' is often a Viking ending referring to a landing place; can you find out what 'thorpe' and 'ham' mean?

The children might be familiar with Roman names, such as Chester or Gloucester.

You can extend this exploration by trying to discover what town names in other countries mean, for example in Australia, New Zealand or the USA. For example:

Pittsburgh—after William Pitt

Philadelphia—brotherly love

Songs of praise to a faithful God

Focus

The Psalms are sometimes songs, sometimes not. This session will look at the way the Psalms are written—and then we'll write our own!

Music! Wow! On pages 3–9 of *Tiptoes and Fingertips*, we met David, who wrote some of the Psalms. He wrote some really cool stuff...

Scene Setter

Psalm 150 is a great psalm; not only does it show us a good way of praising God, it also tells us something about ancient Hebrew music.

Discussion Starters

Start by reading the psalm with the children and then follow this with a discussion about what everyone thinks of when they think of music. Talk about different styles of music—give some examples if you have the facilities to do so.

- ☉ **What would your top ten be?**
- ☉ **Discuss the difference between music and words. When we talk of 'songs' we often confuse the two.**
- ☉ **Discuss also the purposes of music: for example, songs composed for dancing or marching.**
- ☉ **What do the different instruments mentioned in the psalm sound like? You might be able to find examples. (You could listen to Britten's *Young Person's Guide to the Orchestra*; various versions are available.)**

Activities

Making instruments

Children enjoy making instruments. There are two basic sorts of instrument: pitched, which have notes that can play tunes (chimes, pipes, guitar), and unpitched, which present different sounds (drums, claves, maracas). Even these instruments do, of course, have pitch—different sized claves will make higher or lower pitches.

In general it is easier to make unpitched instruments, so we will concentrate on these. Think about how to make sounds with the instruments, by shaking or striking, for example. Here are some suggestions, you will probably have met some of them before!

We made some of these instruments at school—what a row!

Pot shakers

Shakers can be made with all sorts of different containers, although yogurt pots are not actually very satisfactory as the plastic does not resonate well. Experiment with containers made of glass, wood or metal and with different things inside them. You might like to try rice, sand, marbles, or chick-peas, for example, or a mixture of different items.

How and why are the sounds different?

Which one do you think is most interesting?

Claves

The sound will change with the material used. Wood is the most common—rosewood makes very good claves. Again, experiment: start off with an old broom handle. What happens if you drill a few holes in the sticks?

Crown cork shakers

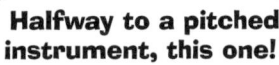

This is the old standby tambourine, but you'll need adult help to make it.

Crown corks (beer bottle tops) can be bought in bags from winemaking or brewing shops—you don't have to drink anything to get them! Drill holes in the centre and attach to a stick by passing a nail through the hole and hammering it into the stick. Try different numbers of crown corks on the nails, or try using hollow sticks. What happens if you mix washers and crown corks on the same stick?

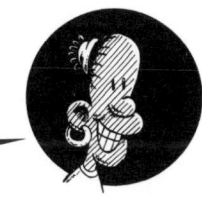

Bamboo harps

Halfway to a pitched instrument, this one!

Simply cut different lengths of bamboo and then push a skewer or something similar through each piece to remove the pith. Next, string the pieces together as shown and strike the instrument with another piece of bamboo. Experiment to see whether or not it makes a difference if the striker is hollowed out.

Whilst you will hear definite pitches or notes with this instrument, it will probably not be possible to play a recognizable tune. To do that you would have to tune it. If you have some musical knowledge you might wish to try this by cutting and testing the bamboo lengths against a piano.

Milk bottle pianos

Fill at least five milk bottles with varying amounts of water. Your milk bottle piano can be easily tuned by adding or subtracting the water in each bottle. Use coloured water to add a touch of interest. If you tune your milk bottles against a piano, it is advisable to use a pentatonic scale—the black notes on the piano—because almost anything that children play will then sound like a tune. An ordinary major scale is not so satisfying.

Making music

Use your instruments to develop an appreciation of the way that sounds are put together.

Although the instruments you have made will not be long-lasting, they are a good introduction to using instruments in the group. Encourage those who play an instrument to bring their instrument along—make sure the instruments are well looked after during the session. Over a period of time you might be able to build up an orchestra or band!

Start by singing a simple song and then adding instruments to it.

★ **Claves—simply play the pattern of the words**

★ **Drum (tapped with fingers)—play the beat of the song (ONE two three four, ONE two three four, etc.)**

★ **Tambourine—gently shake to emphasize important words**

★ **Chime bars—these can play the main letter of any chord symbol; for example, if the chord symbol is B, then play the B chime bar. If the symbol is more complex, for example, Bmaj7, then just play the letter (in this case B).**

★ **On the chime bars, sharp and flat notes are likely to be black. They will all have two notes written on them, for example, G#/A♭.**

This activity can be developed by changing the instruments with each verse, or by adding instruments to build up a climax. If the song has a chorus then you might increase the instruments used for that.

To build this further, you can use *ostinato*, which is a short section of rhythm or tune which is repeated throughout the song. The drum is actually playing *ostinato* in the above suggestions, but not very interestingly.

If you have two drums, then one can play the beat and the other a variation of it, like this:

Beats	1	2	3	4
Drum 1	X	X	X	X
Drum 2	X	x x	X	0

X = 1 beat   x = half a beat (a quick note)
0 = a rest

Children will be able to use this way of writing the beat quite easily to invent their own *ostinato* patterns. Encourage them to experiment. Music develops and grows as it is practised. Encourage the children to work at their practice so that they are pleased with the finished result.

A musical procession

Look at Psalms 120 to 134. This group of psalms is sometimes known as the 'songs of ascent'. It is believed that they were used by pilgrims as they ascended Mount Zion during the great temple festivals.

Discuss together how the style of the music might have changed as the pilgrims got closer and closer to the temple. Spend a little time talking about festivals that we celebrate in our churches and our homes. You may also wish to mention different kinds of pilgrimage, why people go on pilgrimage and the sorts of places that they go to.

Divide into groups and ask each group to make up some music for the various stages in the ascent. They could even choose a short passage from one of the appropriate psalms (120–134) to go with it. In your discussions mention the tiredness of pilgrims, the heat of the day, or the cool of the evening and the rising excitement as the pilgrims approached the temple. You might also like to mention specific sounds: rustling clothes, sandalled feet, many voices and the presence of the animals. There might also be ritual noises, such as fanfares and the opening of temple doors.

Ensure that the children are discerning in the types of sounds that they use and are disciplined in their use of instruments.

Give the children approximately ten minutes to think about the music they want to make and then bring everyone back together and see what the whole 'sound picture' sounds like.

Drawing Together

The Psalms are a great resource for prayer as well as for songs.

Ask the children to find the book of Psalms in their Bibles and to spend a little time choosing part of a psalm to use as a prayer. The children might like to do this in pairs. Be aware of any reading difficulties and give assistance where appropriate.

Now share the songs, rhythms and tunes that you have been working on together. Between the pieces of music, ask the children to read out the section of a psalm that they have chosen as their prayer.

End by reading Philippians 2:6–11, a New Testament equivalent to a hymn or psalm of praise.

Jesus' childhood and baptism

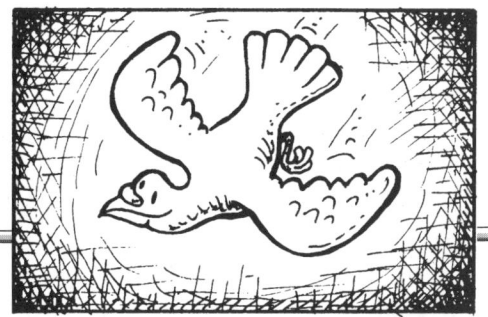

Focus

We do not have much information about Jesus' childhood. It is important to emphasize this point as many myths have been formed in hymns and popular culture depicting Jesus as meek, mild and obedient. Yet none of this is found in the Bible itself and much of it comes from the moral sensibilities of the Victorian era.

We learnt about this in Families and Feelings—pages 18–24.

Yes! And we met two people who had seen Jesus as a baby in the temple on pages 52–57 of Searchlights and Secrets.

Scene Setter

Choose either Jesus' childhood or baptism and ask the children to use their Bibles to answer one of the two questions below.

- ◎ **What are we told about Jesus' childhood in the gospels?**

- ◎ **What do we know of Jesus' baptism from the gospels?**

Jesus' childhood

The childhood of Jesus can be found in the following passages:

MATTHEW 2:13–15 AND 19–23.

Matthew's account focuses on his use of Old Testament prophecy. He appears to use two quotations, but whilst the first (2:15) is from Hosea 11:1, the second is not a direct Old Testament quotation, as is indicated by the use of the plural 'prophets' in verse 23.

Mark does not mention Jesus' childhood at all but does record that he came from Nazareth (1:9 and 24).

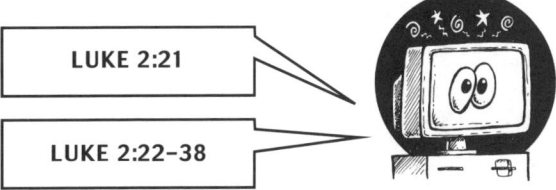

LUKE 2:21

LUKE 2:22–38

There are three parts to Luke's account. The presentation in the temple and the sacrifice are a sign of obedience to the Law—the sacrifice may also indicate the relative poverty of Jesus' family, as indicated by Leviticus 12:8. Notice that it is Mary who is being purified, not Jesus.

It is worth noting the role of the Holy Spirit in the story of Simeon. Read the story with the children, up to and including verse 35.

The record of Anna is shorter, but again there is recognition of Jesus' significance.

LUKE 2:41–52

The boy Jesus in the temple. This is the only story of Jesus' childhood beyond his infancy. This story gives us some clues as to Jesus' understanding of himself, but it does not really give any indication about his family life. Notice Mary's 'your father' and Jesus' words 'my Father'. There is an echo of this phrase in Luke 8:19. Verse 51 is not a moral observation that 'Jesus had learned his lesson', rather an observation of the typical family order of the day. Verse 52 makes us think of a rather handsome figure. Bring the children's attention to the words, 'His mother treasured all these things in her heart.' How do these words compare with Luke 2:19?

Jesus' baptism

Jesus' baptism appears in all four gospels. It is interesting to look at all of them. There are two main points which are common to all four accounts.

1. **The preaching and mission of John. John is the only prophet in the whole of the Bible who speaks *of* and *to* the Messiah. As cousins, it is likely that Jesus and John had already met each other before Jesus' baptism.**

2. **The coming of the Holy Spirit as a dove. This image is well known in art history and is always a major clue when trying to tell whether a picture is of the baptism of Jesus or not! Mention of the Holy Spirit could lead into a discussion about the 'dove of peace', but the use of the image of the dove in the gospels is a picture of God's anointing and recognition of his Son, Jesus, not a picture primarily of peace.**

Discussion Starters

If you have been baptized, do you remember your baptism? If you are members of a church which practises adult or believer's baptism, talk with the children about this. Concentrate upon the fact that different Christian traditions are trying to follow the commands of God in Christ just as Jesus and John themselves were doing.

Likewise, talk about different ways that baptism is carried out, for example, by full immersion, or just by sprinkling the water on the forehead and signing the cross. The discussion might form a value observation of the different approaches to the sacrament of baptism and lead the group to a deeper understanding of what baptism is all about.

Activities

Baptism in art

If you are able to find any historical artwork depicting the baptism of Jesus you will see that the descending dove is a prominent feature.

★ **How might we indicate the Spirit of God 'descending' at Jesus' baptism?**

★ **How might we show Jesus surrendering his authority in obedience to God?**

★ **How does this differ from what John had imagined?**

Invite the children to draw a picture of Jesus' baptism, using either bright or contrasting colours, or collage with cloth for the 'earthly' figures and landscape, and foil for the dove.

Encourage the children to use cartoon-style figures, or collage figures cut from magazines, if they find drawing people difficult.

Acting out a baptism

With this theme we have a great opportunity to explore, first hand, one of the most significant aspects of the Christian life. With your group, go through all the stages of a service of baptism and allow members of the group to ask questions as you go. Don't miss out any prayers or readings—do the whole thing. If you wish, invite members of your group to take up the various roles involved, including the role of clergy.

If you can get your minister to be involved, especially to explain the significance of each part of the service, this would be a valuable contribution.

Prayers

Dear Lord,
Jesus was obedient to
your wishes when he was
baptized.
Help us to be obedient to your wishes
for us
and, by learning more of you,
grow closer to you. Amen

Father,
We pray for all those who are being
baptized today.
Give them a growing understanding of
your kingdom.
Be with them always
and keep them in your love. Amen

Drawing Together

Water—our second birth

Set a jug of water and a bowl on a table at the front of the group.

Reader

Water reminds us of Jesus' baptism.

Pour the water into the bowl. If you use a metal bowl it will be clearly heard.

Reader

The sound of water reminds us of the voice of God, speaking to us in the busyness of life.

Dip a finger into the water and touch the child to your left on the forehead with it.

Reader

The feel of water reminds us of God's touch, forever reaching out to us.

Take the bowl around the room, or allow the children to pass it round, and invite each person in the circle to dip a finger in the bowl and touch the person to their left on the forehead. When everyone has done so, say a prayer or sing a song together.

Give each child a plastic cup. Pour a little water from the jug into each cup.

Reader

When we taste the water it reminds us that God gives each of us life.

Invite each person to take a sip.

Finish with a song or a prayer.

Theme Extension

Split the group into four small groups and ask each smaller group to look up the story of Jesus' baptism in one of the gospels—each group chooses a different gospel. Make a list of the events of the story. Make a note of what is being said. What is similar about the four accounts? What is different? Why? What does each gospel tell us about Jesus' obedience?

> MATTHEW 3:13–17
> MARK 1:9–11
> LUKE 3:21–22
> JOHN 1:29–34

Jesus in the desert

Focus

The temptations of Christ are intelligible only from a position of faith. Children are not able, in general, to step outside themselves enough to see from the perspective of faith; neither is it safe to assume that children have a sufficient understanding of what faith is to be able to appreciate the subtlety of the interactions between Jesus and the devil. However, there are many powerful things that can be learned from these passages.

We visited the desert on pages 18–23 of Friends and Followers.

It wasn't very cool... and we're starving!

Scene Setter

LUKE 4:1–13

Jesus returned from the Jordan full of the Holy Spirit and was led by the Spirit into the desert.

This story occurs in only three gospels—the synoptic gospels ('synoptic' means 'through the same eye'). You might like to discuss what kind of eye this is. Why does John not record the story of Jesus in the desert? You won't need to be looking for the *right* answer to this question, but it will serve to highlight that John's gospel is different from the other three.

Mark's account of Jesus in the desert is very short, but it serves to whet the appetite for the longer versions in Matthew and Luke. It is best to use Luke's account for two reasons. First, Luke builds the interaction between Jesus and the devil, with a defined structure to the statements which pass from one to the other. Secondly, Luke closes

his account with the ominous words '...he left him for a while'. This phrase leaves the reader awaiting the reappearance of the devil—and sure enough, he does reappear, for example in Luke 22:3.

Discussion Starters

- What is significant about the fact that Jesus spent time in the desert?
- Talk for a little while about solitude.
- How do you feel if you have to be by yourself for any length of time?

Activities

Same-eye images

You will need shoe boxes or something similar, newspapers, magazines, plain paper, pencils, crayons, glue and scissors.

As mentioned above, 'synoptic' means 'through the same eye'. Talk about what we see through our eyes and what it would be like to look through someone else's eyes.

How did Jesus' and the devil's view of the scriptures differ?

- **Jesus saw through the eyes of God.**
- **The devil saw through the eyes of self.**
- **The devil saw wealth, power, popularity and greed.**
- **Jesus saw obedience and responsibility to God.**

Choose images from magazines to illustrate these ideas. Beware of simply contrasting Jesus' response and the devil's, rather endeavour to explore how God is at the centre of Jesus' reply. Jesus uses the scriptures to point towards God and, in doing so, enables us to see God more clearly.

Use the images to make up two eye boxes as illustrated.

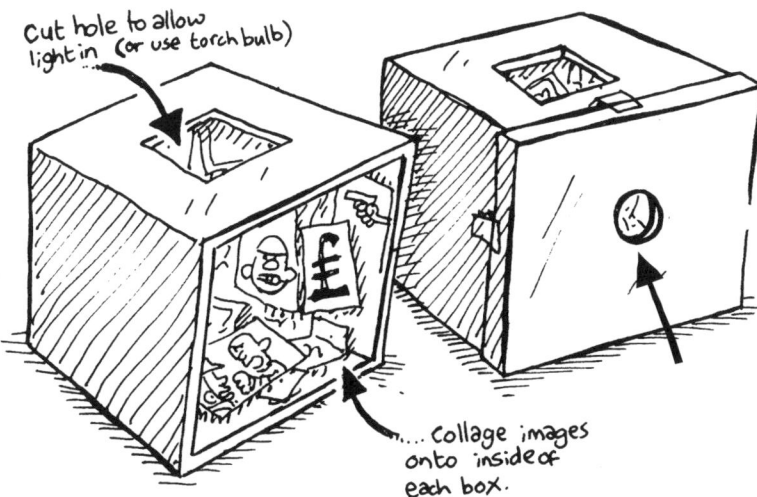

Cut hole to allow light in (or use torch bulb)

Collage images onto inside of each box.

The boxes can be made more exciting by adding a torch bulb fitted to a battery and placed inside the box to light up the contents. The children can decorate the outsides of the boxes to indicate whether it is a box through which we see through Jesus' eyes or a box through which we see through the devil's eyes.

The Christian year

Traditionally, Christians remember Jesus' time in the desert during the season of Lent. This has traditionally been a time of fasting and self-denial. People still talk of giving something up for Lent and often give extra to charities at this time. However, the 'giving something up' concept of Lent was not originally the main purpose of the season—it was a time of preparation leading up to Easter. The concept of self-denial is to allow us to focus more clearly on God and on the work of Christ. The same is true of Advent, which was also a time of fasting and penitence.

Discuss the different seasons of the traditional Christian year: Advent, Christmas, Epiphany, (Candlemas), (Ash Wednesday), Lent, Palm Sunday, Holy Week, Easter, Ascension, Pentecost, Trinity.

Follow the discussion by copying the cycle illustration on to card.

Prayers

Father God,
Help us to see you
through the words you have spoken
in the Bible,
and through the lives of your people
in the Church.
Help us to see things
as you would wish us to see them,
and to live our lives
as you would wish us to live them.
Amen

Dear Lord,
There are many bad things that happen
in your world.
Help us to know the difference between
right and wrong.
Help us to love and care for others as
you would want us to.
Help us to see Jesus in everything we do,
to see the things that you want us to.
Amen

Dear Lord,
When we are alone, or sad,
when we are angry or afraid,
help us remember your words
and not be tempted to choose to be led
away from you. *Amen*

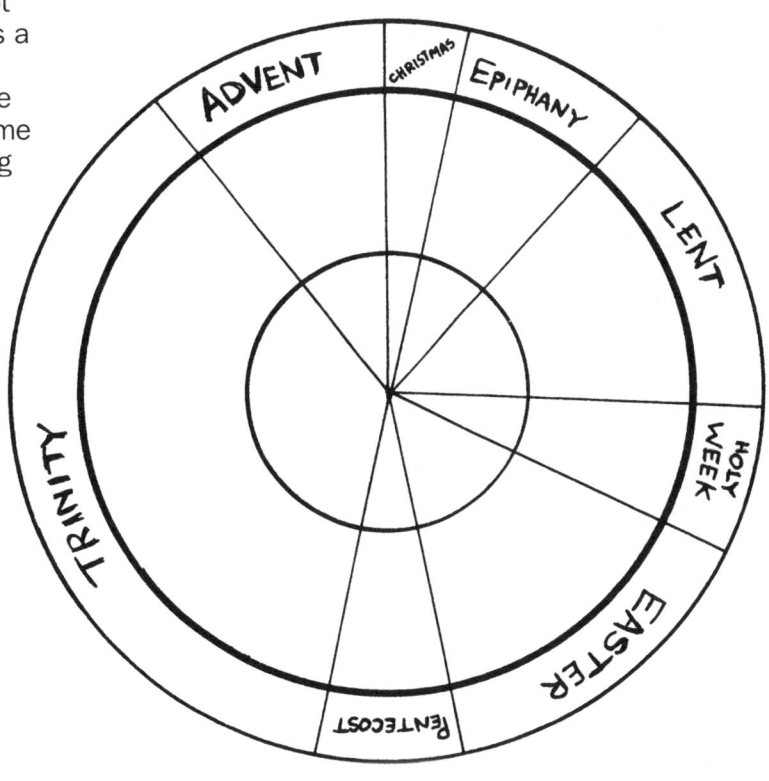

Drawing Together

The power of silence and solitude

Give everyone a large piece of paper and invite the children to think about what it feels like to be alone.

After a short pause, ask everyone to draw something they thought of. When everyone has finished, ask each person to place their drawing in a space on the floor and then gather together in one part of the room.

Leader

In the Old Testament we read about Jonah, who, like Jesus, spent time alone, time when he felt that God was not with him; yet he still did not lose sight of God.

Here is the prayer that he prayed:

Reader   Jonah 2:2–9

When the reading is over, invite each child to find his or her picture and sit beside it. Then, with eyes closed, everyone thinks about what they have drawn and prays a silent prayer about their picture. After a minute everyone picks up their picture and comes back together again.

Finish by saying a prayer together, singing a song or using a grace.

Theme Extension

Through whose eyes?

With an older group you may like to extend the idea of looking though different eyes.

Through whose eyes do we see Jesus? Matthew's, Mark's, Luke's, John's?

This gives an opportunity to use some of the cross-references in Bibles to follow this up and find differences and similarities in the gospels.

What do we see only through the eyes of:

★ Matthew?

★ Luke?

★ Mark?

For example:

⊚ **The parable of the Good Samaritan only appears in Luke's Gospel. Are there any other parables which appear in only one gospel? Why do you think this is?**

⊚ **Jesus' commandment to go to all people everywhere and make them his disciples only appears in Matthew (28:19). Why do you think this is?**

⊚ **How do the resurrection accounts in the three gospels differ?**

You may like to make a striking display to show some of the differences in the three synoptic gospels.

Finally, explore in what way John's gospel is different from the other three. What is missing? What is included that is unique to John? You might like to use the seven 'I am' sayings of Jesus as a basis for your exploration.

Calendar Link

Lent is still one of the best known of the Christian seasons. You may like to hold a pancake party, but do point out that Shrove Tuesday is not really part of the season. The idea of visiting church to be shriven (to confess and receive absolution) is not generally well known. However, this practice became the first part of the preparation of Lent. Your group might enjoy holding a pancake party—they are great fun! If you have one, make sure that everyone understands the purpose of the party: namely, that it is part of the preparation which helps us to take less notice of ourselves so that we may more easily focus on God.

Follow me

Focus

Being a disciple is not always easy. This section introduces the group to what it means to be called by Jesus. The story of the calling of the disciples has been taken from Matthew's gospel. Matthew relates the story without the miracle of the catch of fish, and the children can be encouraged to think about what it means to follow Jesus without the evidence of a miracle to help us in our decision.

Boot took us to meet Simon Peter and Andrew in Friends and Followers.

Yep! That was on pages 24–31.

Scene Setter

MATTHEW 4:18–22

'Come with me, and I will teach you to catch people.'

This short passage has a lovely simple pastoral feel to it. Encourage the children to think themselves into the scene with the sights, sounds and smells of the lakeside, the lapping water and the fishermen busy at their nets. After reading Matthew's account together, spend a few minutes reflecting on what time of day it might have been and the atmosphere of a lakeside.

Discussion Starters

Start by discussing the fact that nowadays we must never go with strangers—no one should ever expect us to drop everything and follow them. So we're going to look at why the fishermen responded to Jesus' call to them and how that same call still comes to us today.

★ What do you think it was about Jesus that made the fishermen take notice of what he said to them?

◎ What were Simon and Andrew giving up to go with Jesus?

★ Was Jesus a stranger to them?

◎ What would my response have been if I had been one of the fishermen?

★ What is my response today?

Activities

Fishing nets

You'll need a real fishing net, or an old tennis or badminton net, paper or thin card, pens, scissors, paints, glue, magazines and photographs of the missionaries attached to your church or information leaflets from a missionary society.

This activity helped us to think about what 'misson' means.

MATTHEW 10:5–10

'Go and preach, "The Kingdom of heaven is near!"'

Cut fish shapes from the card. These could include octopus and crayfish as well as the conventional fish shapes! Invite the children to find pictures of people in the magazines to cut out, or to draw and paint their own and stick on to the fish shapes. Mount the pictures on the net—if you poke them through the holes it will look as if they have indeed been 'caught'! If you are able to include items such as pieces of seaweed, floats, fishing rods and reels, they will add to the impact of the display. Mount the photographs of your church missionaries or the information leaflets amongst the fish shapes.

Ask the children to draw pictures of themselves and add them to the display. Do they see themselves as the fish or the fishermen?

Packing our bags

This activity helped us to think about what we need to follow Jesus.

You will need a selection of items that you might take on a trip, for example, a map, a compass, food and drink, a torch and clothing.

See if you can find a verse in the Bible which would be appropriate for each of the items that you might take with you. You might want to use a concordance to do this. Here are some suggestions to get you started:

Food...   **I am the bread of life (John 6:35)**

Drink...   **Whoever is thirsty should come to me (John 7:37–38a)**

Torch ...   **I am the light of the world (John 8:12)**

Map ...   **I am the way (John 14:6)**

Can you find any more?

Games

Magnetic fishing!

Try to catch the disciples...

This is a good way to learn the names of the disciples.

You will need card on which to trace the figure shape, paper clips, small magnets, dowelling sticks, string and a sheet or length of material to represent the edge of the lake.

Make up some card figures of the disciples using one of the lists in Matthew (10:1ff), Mark (3:13ff), or Luke (6:12ff). Make up several figures of some of the disciples and only one of others, and write the names of the disciples on the figures. Attach paper clips to the figures and make up the fishing rods.

Organize the group into teams according to the number of rods you have (one per team). Use two people to hold the sheet and place the figures behind it. Each team sends one person at a time to fish for the fishers.

Play the game over a limited time. The team with the most disciples at the end wins. Players have to throw back any duplicate figures that they fish out. If a team gets all twelve disciples, then they win outright and the game ends.

The day we met Jesus— a drama

This drama is designed to enable the children to think about what the daily life of the disciples might have been like before they met Jesus. Encourage the group to use their imaginations in building up the personalities of each of the disciples. You might like to carry out some research into the lives of first-century working people.

Try to build up a presentation of the scene complete with the conversation that might have passed between the disciples about the coming day and what they have been doing during the night—much fishing was done at night, as indeed it still is.

Introduce the figure of Jesus and let the cast act out their individual responses to Jesus' call.

Continue the drama on to the evening meal at, say, Peter's house, where he is trying to explain why he suddenly felt compelled to follow Jesus.

This drama can work well in church as part of a service. It is especially effective if the figure of Jesus is only seen from behind, or the audience only hear the voice of Jesus—this can be done using a PA system if you have one.

Prayers

Lord God,
It is you we follow
when we respond to the call
of your son, Jesus Christ.
Take us by the hand
and lead us, we pray,
safely through our days in this world
and onward to your glory in the next.
Amen

Father God,
The first disciples were
just like us;
puzzled by Jesus, yet willing to
follow him and learn from him.
Help us to do the same
so that we, too, will
become Jesus' disciples. Amen

Our Father,
Following Jesus is often hard
and confusing.
Be with us and help us
to know when to speak
and what to say,
when to help
and what to do.
In Jesus' name. Amen

Drawing Together

Wind and water wait for Jesus

This is a 'sound picture' worship which comes from the idea that the lake itself in the story of the calling of the disciples is, like the rest of creation, waiting for the coming of the Lord.

The group will need some musical instruments to develop this. There is no reason why they cannot bring their own instruments, but be prepared to encourage them to work together to make the 'sound picture'.

Reader
Have you been to the place where the sun comes up,
or the place from which the east wind blows?
(Job 38:24)

Experiment with 'rising' music—the simplest is to use an ascending scale of notes. However, there are other possibilities. The blowing of the wind can be achieved by rubbing a drum or two pieces of sandpaper together. (Don't rub the drum with the sandpaper!)

Reader
The Lord rules over the deep waters;
he rules as king forever. (Psalm 29:10)

The sounds change here to 'water music'. Think of the kinds of sounds that you might hear from lakeside waters. There may be children in your group who have never seen a lake, so you may have to help a bit. Lake Galilee is quite a large lake and can develop sizeable waves and a swell, so don't be too timid in your approach.

A way to begin is to have a few instruments making a gentle background rhythm and then to add sounds such as waves and oar splashes by briefly bringing in other instruments.

Try using instruments with similar sounds, for example metallic or rattling sounds, and use a conductor to make the music rise and fall, and to cue in the other effects.

Reader
The voice of the Lord is heard on the seas...
(Psalm 29:3)

Bring in all of the instruments, from both sections, to a crescendo, then silence, in which we hear:

Reader
Come with me, and I will teach you to catch people... (Matthew 4:19)

End in silence.

This act of worship could easily be adapted to illustrate the stilling of the storm in Matthew 8:23–27, Mark 4:35–41 and Luke 8:22–25, but you would probably have to add some dramatic voices from the disciples and a 'calm lake' effect after the two brief rebukes from Jesus.

Theme Extension

How do we follow Jesus now? This theme extension builds on the **Packing our bags** activity. This is an opportunity to talk about faith and what following the Christian faith might mean. Encourage children to develop their different ideas about what being a Christian or following Jesus might mean.

Bring out the following points:

⊚ **Like the disciples and the churches they founded, it is good to be together, to be able to share in faith and life with the people of God. This is one of the reasons we gather together as a church, but there are other situations where people might feel that they are with other disciples, at school, at brownies/cubs... let the discussion follow its own course; don't press for 'right' answers.**

⊚ **We need to keep Jesus (and God!) in sight if we are to follow successfully.**

⊚ **How do we do this?**

> **Reading the Bible...**
>
> **Praying...**
>
> **Going to church...**

Make a big list of ideas.

Think about the things that can help us, for example, books, pictures, special objects and, of course, more directly perhaps, resources which help explain the Bible, like the *Livewires* books which children can read to discover more about their embryonic Christian faith.

Making an entry

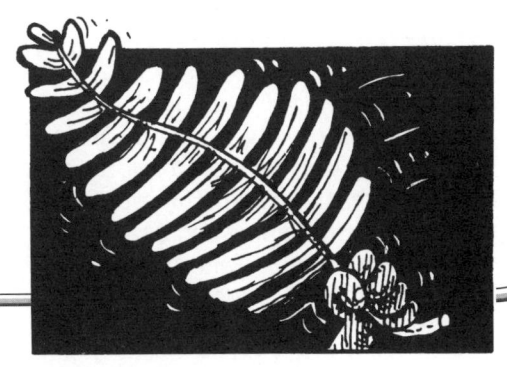

Focus

In the coming of Jesus, the Old Testament meets with the New, and sparks fly as the Pharisees feel increasingly threatened by the disturbing revelation of God. This section stands at the beginning of the Easter cycle, from Palm Sunday through to Holy Week, from the resurrection beyond to the ascension and the wait for the coming of the Spirit. This season is, for most believers, the most important time of the Christian year.

> The crowds and the noise were amazing! We were there in Tiptoes and Fingertips—you can read about our adventures on pages 25–30.

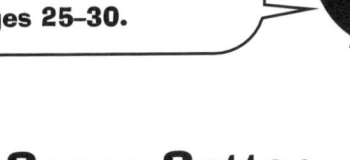

Scene Setter

MATTHEW 21:1–11

> When Jesus entered Jerusalem, the whole city was thrown into an uproar. 'Who is he?' the people asked. 'This is the prophet Jesus, from Nazareth in Galilee,' the crowds answered.

> In order to set the scene in its context, you need to read the story of the Last Supper alongside the description of the entry into Jerusalem.

MATTHEW 26:17–30

These two stories have parallels in the giving of instructions to the disciples, and contrasts in the number of people who greeted Jesus on Palm Sunday compared with the relatively few who attended the Last Supper.

Discussion Starters

When a famous person comes to visit, he or she will quickly be surrounded by a crowd of people—we feel excited at the prospect of their coming.

★ Why are the people happy?

★ What is Jesus' response in Matthew's gospel? And in Luke's? (19:28ff)

★ Is this the kind of thing that makes you excited?

★ What similarities can you find between the triumphal entry and the Last Supper stories? You might like to make lists of these as you find them.

Activities

The Easter road

> This is the first part of three sessions of activity work to produce a single item.

The Easter road is a series of models of scenes from the days of Holy Week. When the scenes have been completed they could be laid out along the aisle of your church, or the floor of your meeting hall, so that people can walk from one scene to the next. The suggestions for making each scene can be adjusted to suit your own ideas and situation.

Before you begin you must decide on the scale of the project, both in terms of its sophistication and its size. For example, the road could be just a couple of metres long, or could be designed to go right round church.

These are the scenes that will make up the whole road:

◎ **The triumphal entry**
◎ **The Last Supper**
◎ **The way to the cross**
◎ **The crucifixion**
◎ **The burial**
◎ **The empty tomb**

(You can add more if you like—such as the anointing at Bethany, or the clearing of the temple.)

The scale you decide on will determine the kind of figures that you use. Three-dimensional figures made from materials such as pipe cleaners or dolly pegs will work better with this project than those made of flat card, especially if people are to walk around it. You may want to try modelling the figures in clay—you might find a friendly school to fire them for you! If you use one of the modern 'no-fire' clays, the models will crumble eventually, but with real clay they will last for many years.

Begin by telling the story of the triumphal entry.

MATTHEW 21:1–11

For the figures you will need pipe cleaners, dolly pegs, clay or card rolls.

For the clothing you will need scraps of material or coloured paper to make cloaks and robes.

You'll also need to make branches and leaves. You could use cloth, paper, or modelling material such as Fimo or salt dough for these.

You can make the town walls by simply cutting card and either drawing on the stone effect or cutting out card stone shapes and sticking them on.

And the gates can be made from real wood, or rolled and painted paper.

The figures can be arranged to illustrate various parts of the story, such as a crowd to suggest the celebration and excitement, or a few people watching Jesus' confrontation with the Pharisees (Luke 19:39–40).

Try illustrating some of the text, for example, '…the stones themselves will start shouting.'

The Last Supper

Read the story together before starting this second part of the road. The children will need to work out which part of the meal to depict. Encourage them to think about what might have been on the table, and in the room itself. Try to move beyond their seeing the supper as just a vague 'tea with the disciples'. Talk about why and how the meal is remembered and re-enacted in the Eucharist.

The same general principles apply with this part of the road as they did for the first part.

This time you will need…

Figures of Jesus and the disciples.

Things to eat—these can be drawn or modelled with Fimo or Plasticine.

A table—how might it have been different from our own dining tables?

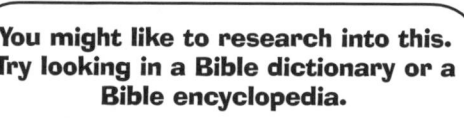

You might like to research into this. Try looking in a Bible dictionary or a Bible encyclopedia.

What else might have been in the room?

How was it lit?

Were there water jars?

Were the things needed for the foot-washing taken away before the meal was eaten?

Design for Last Supper Scene

Painted Background

model of Jesus

Disciple models

matchbox (with cardboard table top)

cloth

by Di...

The two scenes can stand alone as models in their own right—or be kept to form part of the Easter road project over the next few weeks.

Prayers

Dear Lord,
At your coming,
may we be among those
who lay down our cloaks,
may we be among those who shout
and sing,
may we be among those who call
you king. Amen

Lord Jesus,
Help us to serve you, for you are
our king.
Help us to learn what it means to serve,
as you taught your disciples.
Be with us, we pray, as we take the
message of your coming to the world.
Amen

Drawing Together

Jesus is coming—a rather noisy interpretation

You might need to practise this!

Split into groups and give each group a short phrase from the shouts of the crowd, such as 'God bless the king', 'Glory to God', 'Praise God', 'Praise to David's son' or any others that are suggested.

Each group now spends a few minutes learning to 'clap' the syllables of the words. They will have to agree on which syllables are long and which short; for instance, 'God bless the king' could be 'long—long—short—long', or 'short—long—short—long'. It doesn't matter as long as all the children agree to use the same beat. Once they have sorted it out you can begin.

Start with a prayer.

Very quietly, group by group begin the rhythms, clapping and whispering the words. Once everyone has joined in, begin to clap louder and louder. (A good way to do this is to start clapping using only one finger and the palm of the hand, then two fingers, then three and so on.) The voices stay at a whisper.

Indicate when you want the clapping and voices to stop—make this a sudden halt.

Reader 1

Command your disciples to be quiet.

Reader 2

I tell you that if they keep quiet, the stones themselves will start shouting.

The groups shout their phrases and then, once again in rhythm, start to clap—loudly at first and then gradually quieter and quieter.

End with a prayer.

Drama or Dance

You might want to develop the entry into Jerusalem with the use of instruments. If you have pitched instruments you might like to make simple tunes to sing the phrases shouted by the crowd. The whole thing could be developed into a carnival, using planned rhythms and tunes. A way to introduce this would be to listen to music from festivals in other parts of the world, for example Rio, Bombay, Tokyo or Dublin.

The Last Supper has been portrayed in art throughout history. You might like to see how many different paintings you can find. You could try looking in your local library or secondhand bookshops for books with good reproductions. You don't need to know anything about art, history, or who the artist was. The two scenes which are most often painted are the washing of feet and the breaking of bread. See if you can tell which character is which in each painting—including the character of Judas.

Calendar Link

This session is designed to mark the beginning of Holy Week. You might like to try and find out how Christians from traditions other than your own, and indeed around the globe, celebrate Holy Week. Easter is the most significant time in the Christian year and it is important to convey this to our children. Unlike Christmas, Easter demands a response in faith, which is not generally acknowledged in the secular world. You might like to discuss the different ways in which the media and shops approach the two seasons.

Sadness and death

Focus

Jesus' death on the cross has a resolution which brings meaning to the events. However, the details of the crucifixion can be a difficult subject to deal with, firstly because it is an intensely personal account, but also because of its political implications. For example, many further crimes have occurred because Christians have persecuted the Jewish people for killing Christ, and Jewish people generally regard the crucifixion of Christ as just another unjust murder of a Jew by a foreign power (however misguided they thought Jesus to be). These two factors are worth considering as you approach the events of Good Friday.

This was scary. We heard about it in Tiptoes and Fingertips.

Yeah, pages 33–37.

Sadness is a very personal emotion and will be experienced differently by each individual. For example, whilst some might find the question 'Why did Jesus die?' easy to answer because they have the assurance of faith, they might find it more difficult to answer the question 'Why did my rabbit die?'

Scene Setter

MATTHEW 27:27–50

followed by...

LUKE 23:44–48

Jesus cried out in a loud voice, 'Father! In your hands I place my spirit!'

These passages have been put together because they bring out the story as it focuses on what is happening to Jesus. The cruelty, the sadness of the disciples and the mysterious portents surrounding the death of Christ—darkness, the torn curtain, the words of Jesus on the cross—are all present. The story of Easter, as with the story of Christmas, has by tradition been pieced together from each of the gospels. There is evidence to suggest that the stories of Christ's passion might have been in existence in the written word before the gospels were written. This would account for many of the similarities which draw the accounts together. After the resurrection, the gospels go their own ways again.

Discussion Starters

As the suggested passages are quite long, you might like to read them through beforehand and create your own précis to describe the events to the group. Make sure you include each of the important events recorded in the passages.

◎ **What is happening in this story?**

★ **How do Jesus' friends react?**

◎ **Do they understand?**

Activities

Continuing the Easter road

The two scenes you need to make this time are Jesus taking his cross to Golgotha (or Simon doing it for him) and the crucifixion scene itself. The road needs to climb a hill, or at least go past one.

For Jesus carrying the cross you need the figures of Christ, the soldiers and the crowd...

...and a cross.

How you make the cross depends on the scale of your road. If you have small figures then two lolly sticks might do, although the cross need not be wooden—you can use one cut from card. Discuss with the children whether they think that the cross would have been made of finished timber or might have been rather rougher. If you have been looking at the art suggestions in these sessions, you could see what kinds of crosses artists have depicted over the years.

Discuss with the children how the crowd in this scene might differ from the crowd in the first scene, the entry into Jerusalem. The first scene was a celebration and the crowd might have been portrayed with bright colours. In this scene the crowd needs to be more sombre. This can be achieved with the use of colour, but also by the posture of the figures. You won't be able to alter the posture if you are using card tube figures, but clay or pipe cleaners give more scope for this.

The crucifixion scene needs very careful thought.

Who would have been present? Discuss with the group how they want to portray the crucifixion. For example, do they want to emphasize the loneliness of Christ at his death (forsaken even by God)? Or do they want to show the contrast between the wailing women, the disciples at the foot of the cross and the gaming of the soldiers? Do they wish to include the two robbers? Let the children decide this between themselves—encourage them to give reasons for their choices.

The hill could be made symbolically with a couple of boxes, or could be more realistically made using papier mâché or Modroc.

The unlit crucifix

This is a very simple display which will help children to appreciate the literal and symbolic darkness of Good Friday.

You will need a crucifix, a plain cross and a box, plus a source of light.

The cross is placed at the back of the box and the crucifix at the front. Between them is a source of light, a torch bulb, for example. When the bulb is lit the empty cross is lit up—the light of the risen Christ—and the crucifix is left in darkness. Children can make their own cross and crucifix if you wish.

If wooden crosses and a non-flammable box are used, a safety candle (nightlight) could provide the light source. Do not leave this unattended.

This can be set up on Good Friday, with the dark crucifix and an unlit candle. The candle can then be lit on Easter Sunday.

Prayers

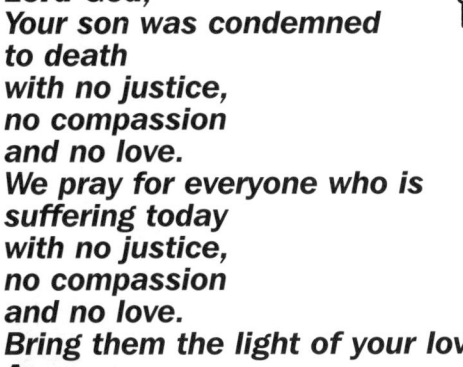

Lord God,
Your son was condemned
to death
with no justice,
no compassion
and no love.
We pray for everyone who is
suffering today
with no justice,
no compassion
and no love.
Bring them the light of your love.
Amen

Dear Father,
We think of those known to us
who are sad.
Help us to show them
that you love them.
Help them to grow
out of their sadness and into
the joy of knowing you. Amen

Drawing Together

Telling stories

This is a very simple act of worship based on the concept of storytelling within village communities. It deals with the coming of hope in sadness and death.

Sit around in a circle with the storyteller in the middle. The following story is given as an example, but others could be used. It is not a parable, but may be used to help broaden the awareness of the importance of stories in understanding our place before God and the work of Jesus.

Reader

Jesus returned to the other side of the lake. The people welcomed him, because they had all been waiting for him. Then a man named Jairus arrived; he was an official in the local synagogue. He threw himself down at Jesus' feet and begged him to come to his home, because his only daughter, who was twelve years old, was dying.

All

Let us praise God for his glorious grace, for the free gift he gave us in his dear Son!
(Ephesians 1:6)

Reader

As Jesus went along, the people were crowding him from every side. Among them was a woman who had suffered from severe bleeding for twelve years; she had spent all she had on doctors, but no one had been able to cure her. She came up in the crowd behind Jesus and touched the edge of his cloak, and her bleeding stopped at once.

All

Let us praise God for his glorious grace, for the free gift he gave us in his dear Son.

Reader

Jesus asked, 'Who touched me?' Everyone denied it, and Peter said, 'Master, the people are all round you and crowding in on you.' But Jesus said, 'Someone touched me, for I knew it when the power went out of me.' The woman saw that she had been found out, so she came trembling and threw herself at Jesus' feet. There in front of everybody, she told him why she had touched him, and how she had been healed at once. Jesus said to her, 'My daughter, your faith has made you well. Go in peace.'

All

Let us praise God for his glorious grace, for the free gift he gave us in his dear Son!

Reader

While Jesus was saying this, a messenger came from the official's house. 'Your daughter has died,' he told Jairus; 'don't bother the teacher any longer.' But Jesus heard it and said to Jairus, 'Don't be afraid; only believe, and she will be well.'

All

Let us praise God for his glorious grace, for the free gift he gave us in his dear Son!

Reader

When he arrived at the house, he would not let anyone go in with him except Peter, John and James, and the child's father and mother. Everyone there was crying and mourning for the child. Jesus said, 'Don't cry; the child is not dead, she is only sleeping.' They all laughed at him, because they knew that she was dead. But Jesus took her by the hand and called out, 'Get up my child!' Her life returned, and she got up at once.

All

Let us praise God for his glorious grace, for the free gift he gave us in his dear Son!

May God's grace be with all those who love our Lord Jesus Christ with undying love.
(Ephesians 6:24)

If your group has enjoyed exploring the Bible in the sessions, the children might like to compare the ways in which the four gospels deal with the events of Good Friday. They should be beginning to see how the accounts complement each other. Older children might be able to compare similarities between the four accounts to discover in what ways they are closer than the two accounts of Christmas.

Your group is probably not the best place to discuss personal matters of bereavement and loss. However, these are very important matters for children. If you wish to pursue these matters a little further, Wendy Duffy's 'Children and Bereavement' (Church House Publishing) is a useful resource.

Children may wish to share with you things in their lives that are sad or difficult for them. These issues need to be handled as a friend, not a counsellor. If you are worried by anything that is said, it is best to talk in private to your minister, church leader or the child's parents to ensure difficult situations are not left unresolved.

Celebration

Focus

The Easter story is the climax of the Christian year, but it does not end there. As the events move on to Ascension and Pentecost it is important to help the children to understand the impact that these events have on Christian faith.

> We met some very happy disciples on pages 39–44 of *Tiptoes and Fingertips*.

Scene Setter

MATTHEW 28:1–9 AND LUKE 24:1–12

Suddenly Jesus met them and said, 'Peace be unto you.' They came up to him, took hold of his feet, and worshipped him.

> These two passages tell the story of the disciples finding out something that Christians have celebrated ever since. But the disciples' first reactions were of puzzlement and fear. It wasn't until they realized what had happened that they could celebrate.

Discussion Starters

Invite the group to tell you some of the things that make them happy. Follow this with things that make them sad.

Discuss the contrast between sadness and joy:

- What makes us sad?
- What makes us joyful?
- How do we express our sadness and our joy?
- What do you feel if you are invited to a party, or if you receive a 'thank you' letter?

Activities

Finishing the Easter road

There are two scenes left to complete our Easter road: the burial and then the resurrection.

The burial scene

Discuss together which figures will be needed for this scene.

Think about the tomb. Do you want to make this with natural things such as twigs, stones and small plants, like an Easter Garden, or would you prefer to make the tomb from card? If you want the model to last over many years you might want to consider using papier mâché and chicken wire, or Modroc.

Decide which of the resurrection accounts you would like to depict. Encourage the children to think about what they are representing. Are they going to have a tender scene between Mary and Jesus, or a group of puzzled and frightened disciples looking around to find Jesus' body?

Once you have discussed the details, you will be ready to construct the scene.

Assembling the road is best done with everyone there so that the whole group feels part of it. The whole thing could form an act of worship with an appropriate prayer and hymn for each scene.

The empty cross

This is a sculpture to which everyone can contribute.

Make a selection of crosses using card, based on the diagram below. Cut holes in each cross and then fix them to a base so that they will stand up. Weave the crosses together as shown. Set up the sculpture and place a light behind it. The light will shine through the holes in the sculpture.

By using a selection of crosses from different countries and traditions, the sculpture will demonstrate that Christ died for all.

I sketched these crosses on a school visit to church.

The material that you make this sculpture from depends on the resources you have available. It is probably simplest to make it from stiff card, but if you have the tools you could use plastic card, perspex, thin plywood or even tin! The whole sculpture should be quite large.

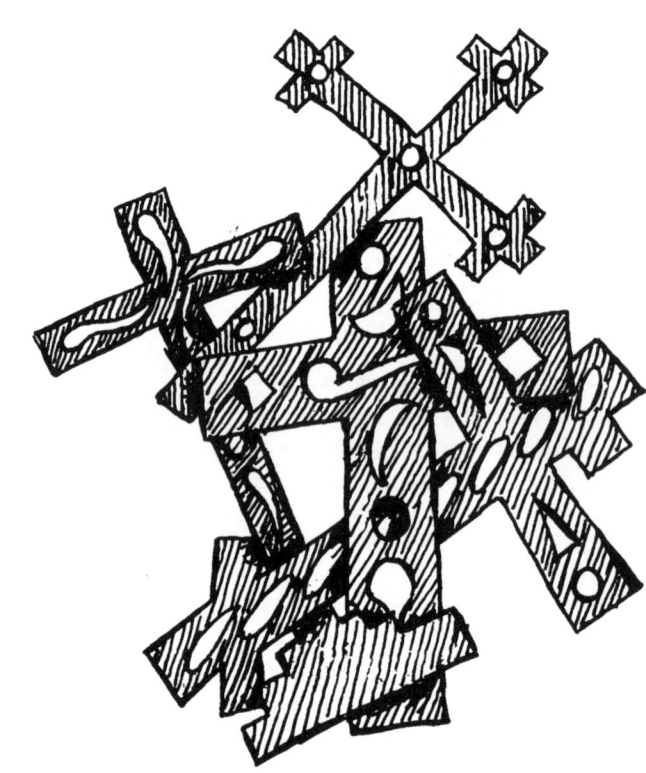

 **Drama**

Meeting Jesus in the garden—what would we say?

This is workshop drama, along the lines of a situation improvization. It is not meant to produce a performance, it is intended to allow the participants to explore their own feelings as they act out the scene, and to begin to empathize with those who were part of that first Easter morning.

Split the group into pairs.

Invite the children to imagine that they are in the garden on that first Easter morning. Ask each pair to choose one person to say the words of Jesus and the other to take the role of one of the women or disciples. Set the scene carefully by reading the account of the burial of Jesus from one of the gospels and creating a suitable, sombre atmosphere. Then invite the pair to play out the scene. Do not allow the scene to go on for long. Encourage those playing the role of one of the women or disciples to decide what to do. Will they hide, tell the others, or run away? How do they feel when Jesus says their name? Try different variations, with the children taking it in turns to play one of the women or disciples and the person saying the words of Jesus. How do they feel if their own name is used instead of the name of one of the women or disciples?

Prayers

This is an antiphonal prayer with the same short acclamation at the beginning and end. The two passages are taken from 1 Peter 1:3 and Isaiah 53:4–6.

All

Let us give thanks to the God and Father of our Lord Jesus Christ!
Because he gave us new life by raising Jesus Christ from death.

Reader

He endured the suffering that should have been ours,
the pain that we should have borne.
All the while we thought that his suffering was punishment sent by God.
But because of our sins he was wounded,
beaten because of the evil we did.
We are healed by the punishment he suffered,
made whole by the blows he received.
All of us were like sheep that were lost,
each of us going their own way.
But the Lord made the punishment fall on him,
the punishment all of us deserved.

All

Let us give thanks to the God and Father of our Lord Jesus Christ!
Because he gave us new life by raising Jesus Christ from death.
Amen

Heavenly Father,
Your word tells us of your mercy to your people,
in the escape from Egypt,
in the building of your temple,
in the words of your prophets,
and in the resurrection of your son.
We praise and thank you for your gift to your people
in the coming of your son, Jesus.
Alleluia!

Drawing Together

Set up a large crucifix and cross on a table in front of the group. Raise the cross up so that it stands higher than the crucifix.

Reader

We remember the darkness and the sadness of Good Friday.

All

We remember the darkness and the sadness of Good Friday.

Reader

We remember Jesus alone on the cross.

All

We remember Jesus alone on the cross.

Reader

Good Friday is past, what do we see?

All

Good Friday is past, what do we see?

Someone walks slowly to the front carrying a single safety candle on a saucer.

Reader

Look, a tiny light coming ever nearer.

All

Look, a tiny light coming ever nearer.

Reader

It is like the tiniest glimmer in the sky at dawn.

All

It is like the tiniest glimmer in the sky at dawn.

Reader

What will we see by the light of this dawn?

All

What will we see by the light of this dawn?

The candle is placed between the two crosses.

Reader

Look at the empty cross.

All

Look at the empty cross.

Reader

The night is over.

All

The night is over.

Reader

The day is come.

All

The day is come.

Reader

Christ is risen.

All

Christ is risen.

All

Alleluia, alleluia!

The litany above, conducted by the children, could be used within a church service.

Calendar Link

Easter

Arrange for the group to be present during the Eucharist in your church and encourage them to observe the way in which Christ's death and resurrection are regularly remembered through the Eucharistic prayer, the bread and the wine.

Follow this with a look at Paul's words in 1 Corinthians 10:16–17 and 11:23–25. You could make up a 'project folder' to show how the different parts of the service relate to the Bible. Compile your research using photographs, drawings and written work.

Summer
TERM

Moses and ten timely tips

Focus

It has been brought to our attention by the media that most people cannot recite the Ten Commandments, the inference being that if we knew them and taught them to our children there would be far fewer problems in our society. Excellent though this premise seems, it unfortunately misses the point, because it takes society as its starting point. The Ten Commandments, however, are not primarily about society, but attitudes to God. Take God out of the centre and we find, to our cost, that society falls apart.

It is vital that every single one of the commandments is seen in the context of the worship of God—not just the first four. When our lives are focused on God, obeying the Ten Commandments will become our spontaneous response.

> You'll find our adventure on Mount Sinai in Searchlights and Secrets.

> It's on pages 10–16. I was really scared!

Scene Setter

> EXODUS 19:16–20
>
> **Moses spoke, and God answered him with thunder.**

The passage prior to the giving of the commandments paints a wonderful picture, with Moses up the mountain in the clouds and the frightened people down below. The sights and sounds of this scene, with the thunder and lightning and the noise of the trumpets, provide an opportunity to fire the imagination and place the giving of the commandments in their biblical context.

Discussion Starters

> EXODUS 20:1–17
>
> **I am the Lord your God.**

> **You might like to use a paraphrase or children's version of the Bible as you read the Ten Commandments together.**

- ◎ Why do we need rules?
- ★ Can you think of any rules which restrict our freedom?
- ◎ Are there any rules which give us more freedom?
- ★ Which of God's rules restrict our freedom, and which give us more freedom?

Activities

What are the Ten Commandments?

Write your own set of commandments, but follow the same pattern: four rules about God and then six about living together as people. These could take the form of 'ten commandments for our club', for example.

When you have done this, discuss how the commandments form a set of social rules contained within our worship of God.

Tablets of stone

> **In this activity we'll be making our own copies of Moses' original stone tablets. Well, nearly!**

You will need two pieces of polystyrene for each child in your group (for example, large, clean meat trays from a supermarket, or polystyrene tiles from a DIY store), scissors, a craft knife (for adult use only!), pencils and marker pens.

The tablets on which the commandments were written have been represented in many shapes over the course of history, though nowadays we generally think of them as being 'gothic' shape. First of all, ensure that the children know what you mean by 'tablet'—it's not a pill you get from the doctor!—and then decide on the shape they wish their tablets to be.

The polystyrene can be cut and then inscribed with a pencil, which makes it look as though the words are carved into it. If you use white polystyrene, it can be coloured with waterproof markers or overhead projector pens.

You'll need to decide on the wording for each commandment and where you want to break the text.

Drama/Mime

The Ten (plus) Commandments

Split the children into groups of three or four and give each group a Bible. Give each group one of the following passages to look up:

Luke 10:25–27

Matthew 28:19–20

John 13:34–35

Ask each group to think of a way in which they could interpret the commandment in the passage with a modern day situation. They can do this through mime, through drama or through drawing.

When everyone has worked out what they are going to do, give them a few minutes to prepare and then ask each group to share their work with the whole group. Discuss which of the Ten Commandments might fit with their interpretation of the passage.

Acting on the commandments

Split the group into ten equal smaller groups and give each small group a slip of paper with one of the commandments written on it, as follows:

1. **Worship no god but me.**
2. **Do not put your trust in false gods.**
3. **Do not use language that dishonours me.**
4. **Set aside a day of rest in each week.**
5. **Respect your parents.**
6. **Do not take away another's life.**
7. **Remain faithful to your husband or wife.**
8. **Do not steal.**
9. **Do not lie.**
10. **Do nothing out of jealousy.**

Invite each small group to work out a mime for their commandment. They then perform their mime to the whole group, who have to guess the commandment.

 ## Games

Invent a game

You will need some coloured card (for example, six cards each of six colours), pencils and scissors.

This activity helps us to see why we need rules.

Divide into groups of three or four and give each group a different coloured card, pencils and scissors. Each group then has to invent a game.

There are no restrictions about the game—it does not have to be competitive, for example—but they will need to work out the rules and be able to tell the rest of the group how to play it.

You could have a vote at the end to decide who has invented the best game.

Prayers

Heavenly Father,
It is often hard to
remember
to do the right thing.
Keep in our minds the way you want us
to live
and be with us as we try to follow you.
Amen

God of all,
Strengthen us to follow
your commands
wherever we may be. Amen

Dear Father,
Help us to put you at the centre of
our lives
and to live according to your
commandments.
Help us to put your son, Jesus, at the
centre of our hearts
and to love according to his
commandments. Amen

Drawing Together

> **This act of worship is like a dance, with words like 'verses' moving around the 'chorus', bringing us back to God again and again.**

Start by designing pictures to illustrate the different lines of the reading. Each picture is then held up as the appropriate words are read out. If you wish, the litany could be used as part of a church service, with the pictures drawn on to acetate sheets and displayed on an overhead projector.

All
Hear the words of the Lord,
'I am the Lord your God... worship no god but me.'

Reader
You made the rainbow as a sign of your promise to Noah.

All
You are our God, we have no god but you.

Reader
You promised Abraham descendants as countless as the stars.

All
You are our God, we have no god but you.

Reader
You led Moses and the people of Israel out of the land of Egypt.

All
You are our God, we have no god but you.

Reader
You brought your word to the people and the kings through the great prophets.

All
You are our God, we have no god but you.

Reader
You brought your people back to their land from distant exile.

All
You are our God, we have no god but you.

Reader
You fulfilled all your promises in your Son, our Lord, Jesus Christ.

All
You are our God, we have no god but you.

Reader
You strengthened your church by the gift of your Holy Spirit.

All
You are our God, we have no god but you.

Reader
Your Son will return, as your word promises.

All
You are our God, we have no god but you.

All
Hear the words of the Lord,
'I am the Lord your God... worship no god but me.'

> **When we did this, we chose a different person to do each of the readings.**

Jesus teaches about lifestyle

Focus

It is important for us to recognize the difference between right and wrong and to understand how our behaviour affects the way we live. In this session we will focus both on what Jesus taught about lifestyle, and how he saw lifestyle as something more than just another set of rules.

We heard Jesus teaching about lifestyle in Searchlights and Secrets—he told us some great stories that really turned us upside-down!

Yep! That was on pages 31–44 of our adventure.

Scene Setter

Jesus did not teach in a vacuum. His teaching is part of the 'fulfilment' of the law of God. Sometimes he taught in the context of the Jewish people's relationship to their religion and to God. At other times his teaching was a specific response to questions about lifestyle, as in the parable of the Good Samaritan.

MATTHEW 6:25–33

'...be concerned above everything else with the Kingdom of God and with what he requires of you.'

Jesus teaches us that it is our attitude towards God which must lie at the heart of our Christian faith. Lifestyle is not about striving after 'good works', it is about giving ourselves completely to him from whom everything else flows.

Discussion Starters

★ **What do we like about life?**

★ **What do we dislike?**

★ **Whose lifestyle do we find attractive?**

★ **Would we like to be that person and why?**

★ **Is there a difference between someone's 'life' and their 'lifestyle'?**

Activities

My kinda life...

You'll need a selection of magazines or newspapers (including those aimed at children), glue, paper and scissors.

Start by discussing the children's lives with them and exploring the question, 'What is *my* lifestyle?'

Go on to find illustrations of different lifestyles in the magazines and newspapers. You might find, for example, the life of a model, a sports personality, fictional superhero, or a mother. Are there any striking gender differences in the examples you have found. Why do you think this is? Do you think they are right?

Move on to discuss the 'trappings' that go with a chosen lifestyle—bear in mind that it is quite possible for people to have 'multiple' lifestyles.

What are the ideals which go with different lifestyles?

◎ **Wealth?**

◎ **Security?**

◎ **Popularity?**

Cut out pictures to represent these things: cheering crowds, flashy cars etc. Assemble them into a montage.

Using the Bible passage above, talk about whether the images that the group have built up correspond with what Jesus teaches us about lifestyle.

Finish by discussing your own images of what Jesus is talking about. It is quite possible that the two things will tie in together—for example, some of the modern 'superheroes' are incredibly moral, and are good examples of 'secret' charity.

A lifestyle mobile

You'll need thin card, scissors, glue and long lengths of cotton.

This mobile is very simple; there are just three levels and each is equally sized. The grass forms the lowest level, then flowers, then birds, and finally add a Bible verse at the base of the mobile, below the three levels.

Copy the illustrations on to card and cut out enough for each child to have two templates of each item. When everyone has coloured their templates, glue them back-to-back with a length of cotton between them, long enough to run through the whole mobile. Place the grass at the bottom, the flowers in the middle and the birds at the top. Finish by adding a card with one of the following Bible verses written on it:

★ **'Look at the birds: they do not sow seeds, gather a harvest and put it in barns; yet your Father in heaven takes care them!' (Matthew 6:26)**

★ **'Look how the wild flowers grow: they do not work or make clothes for themselves. But I tell you that not even King Solomon with all his wealth had clothes as beautiful as these flowers.' (Matthew 6:28–29)**

★ 'It is God who clothes the wild grass—grass that is here today and gone tomorrow... Won't he be all the more sure to clothe you?' (Matthew 6:30)

You could decorate the card as well.

The Beatitudes — a dramatic interpretation

Divide the group into twos and threes and give each small group a verse from the Beatitudes in Matthew 5:3–12. Ask each group to create a short, improvized drama of their verse.
Each group can perform their improvizations to the others, who act both as critics and audience. Ask them to respond to the drama and explain how, if at all, the drama expressed the meaning of the verse. Give guidance and encouragement as the children express their interpretation of the meaning of the verses.

Prayers

Start by reading the Lord's Prayer from Matthew 6:9–15.

Father in heaven,
You care for us and want the best for us.
Forgive us for not always remembering this
and for often blaming you when we find things hard.
Help us always to remember the words of Jesus that tell us of your love. Amen

Dear Lord,
You have made us
and given us life.
Give us the strength to live our lives as you intend;
and always to share your truth with those around us. Amen

Drawing Together

In this act of worship you need to choose one of the group to be the 'traveller'.

Start with a song and perhaps a prayer. Invite the 'traveller' to come to the front and prepare a pack for him or her to take on their journey.
Lay each item out as you say the words.

Item One	A Bible
Reader	Take a Bible as your guide.
Item Two	A cross
Reader	Take a cross as your passport.
Item Three	Bread
Reader	Take bread as a reminder that God goes with you.
Item Four	Wine
Reader	Take wine as a reminder that Christ goes before you.
Reader	Take all these things and stay true to the life that Christ has given you. Now go!

The traveller leaves and there is silence.

Finish by saying the Lord's Prayer together.

Zacchaeus

Focus

Luke begins Zacchaeus' story with the healing of the blind beggar. The people hear of the coming Christ and gather expectantly to see him. Yet it is not any of these people whom Jesus has come to see, but Zacchaeus. The crowd grumble. But in Jesus' encounter with this man, we find an echo of the return of the prodigal son—the story of Zacchaeus is both a miracle and a parable, and in the end salvation comes.

We sat up in the tree with Zacchaeus.

Me too! On pages 46–51 of Searchlights and Secrets.

Scene Setter

LUKE 19:1–10

'Salvation has come to this house today.'

This story explores the way that people respond to Jesus—not just the response of those who believe or who come to believe, but also the response of 'the crowd' who witness the encounter. Read the story together.

Discussion Starters

★ What would make me change the way that I live my life?

★ What made Zacchaeus change?

Drama

The whole of this session is based on a dramatic interpretation of the story of Zacchaeus. Prepare by discussing together how the story breaks down, for example:

1. **Fuss in the town because Jesus is coming.**

2. **Zacchaeus unable to see.**

3. **Zacchaeus' solution.**

4. **Jesus' recognition of Zacchaeus.**

5. **Zacchaeus comes down—Jesus goes with him.**

6. **The unrest of the crowd.**

7. **The meal and Zacchaeus' declaration.**

8. **The crowd's response.**

Go on to discuss the ways in which the crowd can be used as a foil to the action.

The cast

- Naomi and Esther—two women of the town
- Stephen—Esther's son
- Zacchaeus—the hated tax collector
- Jesus
- Four people from the crowd
- Various townspeople, traders, buyers, travellers etc.

The stage is empty apart from the 'tree'. You can be as ambitious as you like, but a fairly simple tree can be made by stapling a piece of corrugated card to the side of a low stepladder—you'll only need three treads for it to work.

The crowd begin by coming on to the stage and establishing the action. The scene is a marketplace, so some are traders, others are buying.

Esther:
Do you know, I think that Jesus might be coming to Jericho.

Naomi:
Oh, I'm sure that can't be true... preachers are always so busy.

Esther:

Yes, I know, but my sister lives in Jerusalem…

Naomi:

I hate Jerusalem, it's so noisy…

Esther:

…*she* said that she'd heard it from one of his close friends.

Naomi:

Oh, I say, that would be exciting! We've not had a preacher here for ages.

Stephen:

Mum! Mum!

Esther:

What is it? What's the matter?

Stephen:

It's that man, Jesus—he's just made Simon the beggar better!

Naomi:

What! Blind Simon?

Stephen:

Yes! And now Jesus is coming into town.

As Stephen finishes speaking, the crowd begin to murmur words like, 'It's Jesus!', 'He healed Simon!', 'He's coming!', 'Look!' etc. Their voices get louder and louder, as if approaching from a distance. Zacchaeus enters.

Stephen:

Ugh, look Mum, it's that creepy bloke from the big house.

Naomi and Esther:

Oh, it's Zacchaeus, the tax collector.

Zacchaeus:

Morning, Esther; morning, Naomi.

The women ignore him. Zacchaeus moves towards the crowd and tries to speak to some of them. He is ignored. The crowd begin to line up at the side of the stage. Stephen and the women have joined them and only Zacchaeus is left facing the audience. The crowd jostle and peer in the direction from which Jesus will enter.

Zacchaeus:

(to the audience) This is always happening to me. They don't like me 'cos I collect their taxes. Well, someone has to do it—and if I pocket a bit extra for myself—well, that's the perks of the job, isn't it?

Anyway, there hasn't been a crowd this big in Jericho since the last time that Jesus came to town. I remember it well, because I got knocked down in the rush. Sometimes it's no fun being so small!

The crowd begin to call out Jesus' name.

Zacchaeus:

It's Jesus again! This time I'm going to see him! Now what can I do?

(He starts to pace about the stage, looking for inspiration.)

Zacchaeus:

I'll either have to wriggle my way to the front of the crowd *or* I'll have to grow.

(He paces up and down.)

Zacchaeus:

I know! I'll jump up and down!

Zacchaeus begins jumping up and down at the back of the crowd. He shouts out 'Jesus! Jesus!' Every time he does this, one of the crowd turns and tells him to go away, or pushes him. Eventually he is pushed over and he wrenches himself up into a kneeling position. He is under the tree.

Zacchaeus:

Well, that didn't work. I'm going to have to find something to stand on. Yes, that's it, get something big to stand on. Now what can I use? A box… A log… A chair… My cousin…

Zacchaeus can act this out as appropriate. The audience might well join in, 'panto'-style, to tell him to climb the tree. He must finish by noticing the tree.

Zacchaeus:

It's a tree! A tree is big—I'll climb it.

Zacchaeus climbs the tree and looks over the crowd. The noise from the crowd grows now and they begin to move so that they surround the tree. Take care that they don't knock it down! Jesus enters and walks right past the tree, being followed by the crowd. He slowly walks across the stage, pausing to speak to members of the crowd. The audience cannot hear what he says.

   As Jesus approaches the tree, he pauses and looks up. The crowd go silent and freeze.

Jesus:

Hurry down, Zacchaeus, because I must stay in your house today!

Zacchaeus climbs down, a beaming smile on his face.

Zacchaeus:

Oh, Jesus, that will be nice. I do so like guests and no one in this town ever comes to see me—I'm always the one who has to do the visiting, to make them pay their taxes. It would be wonderful to have a guest to whom I can show off my lovely house. Come, sir, this way! Oh, I'm so glad that you chose my house…

Zacchaeus carries on like this as he and Jesus leave the stage in the same direction that Jesus entered. This leaves the crowd stranded at one side. As soon as Zacchaeus' voice disappears, the crowd begin to move around.

Person 1:

Well, if that doesn't just take the biscuit!

Person 2:

Yeah, who does Zacchaeus think he is?

Person 3:

Too right, why should a preacher like Jesus want to go to tea with Zac the Tax Grabber? He's nothing but a cheat!

Person 4:

And now he's cheated us out of Jesus, too!

Person 1:

OK, let's go round to Zacchaeus' place and sort him out.

Person 2:

Yeah, I think that Jesus ought to know just what an old money-grabbing sinner Zacchaeus is!

Person 3:

And we'll be the ones to tell him.

Person 4:

Come on, then…

The crowd leave, following the four speakers. As soon as they have gone, Jesus and Zacchaeus come back on and sit down. They are eating. We hear nothing of anything that they say, the crowd reappear and stand behind Zacchaeus and Jesus.

Person 1:

This man is a sinner!

Person 2:

He has stolen our money!

Person 3:

He has broken his promises to God!

Person 4:

He has no right to have you as a guest!

Zacchaeus:

(speaking to Jesus) Sir, they are right. I have done all those things and worse. But I want to put things right! I will give half of all I own to the poor and, if anyone has been cheated by me, I will pay back four times as much.

Jesus:

(to the crowd) Now see, this house has been saved, for this man, like you, is a descendant of Abraham and was lost.

The Son of Man came to seek and save the lost.

Everyone freezes while Jesus leaves. The crowd start to drift away, leaving Zacchaeus alone. Just as the last person leaves, Stephen runs back and grabs Zacchaeus' hand.

Stephen:

Come on, Zacchaeus…

They leave together.

Prayers

Dear Lord,
We are like Zacchaeus
for we are often selfish and proud.
Help us to turn around
and ask for your forgiveness. Amen

Lord Jesus,
Give us the desire to call out to you.
Give us eyes to look up
to the tree where you died for us.
As we take in what you have done
for us,
help us to give out to others
so that we and they
might be lost no more. Amen

Daniel and God's faithfulness

Focus

The whole story of Daniel is a tremendous tale, full of incident. This session picks up the account of Daniel in the lion's den and highlights a few lesser-known points in this well-known tale.

We met Daniel right at the beginning of Trackers and Trainers. I think Boot was in a dream!

Scene Setter

The story of Daniel and the lions is as much about the king, Darius, as it is about Daniel. And, of course, more about God than either of them! When you have read the story with the children, briefly discuss the cruel conspiracy of the king's advisers and Darius' reaction when Daniel was saved; in particular, his royal command in verses 25–28 of chapter 6.

DANIEL 6:23

...they pulled him up and saw that he had not been hurt at all, for he trusted God.

This story is full of action and excitement and you might want to read it from a dramatized version of the Bible—or work out your own dramatization. Make sure that the group do not lose sight of God as they get caught up in the adventure. It is easy for us to get carried along with the tide of the adventure when we work for God, and to lose sight of who we are working for—Daniel gives us an object lesson in *not* doing just that!

Discussion Starters

Think about bravery for a moment; was Daniel being brave, or did he know that God would save him?

How brave are we?

★ Do we need to be brave when we are working for God?

What protection does faith give to us as Christians?

Activities

Sock puppets

Sock puppets are useful when there are a lot of words—their mouths are very handy!

And they make good lions because they can really bite!

You need enough socks to make the following characters...

★ Darius

Several advisers

★ Daniel

Several lions

Sock puppets can be very simple—just eyes and a mouth—or you can develop them in several ways. The easiest way is to add a 'ruff'. This can be made of card and sits around the neck of the puppet (the wrist of the puppeteer). Colours can identify characters and they can be made richer (for kings) with sequins or foil. Lions can have big, spiky yellow manes. You might like also to add a crown for a king and cloaks that hang from the neck of the puppet.

The green-eyed monster!

Darius' advisers were jealous of Daniel—what makes us jealous?

> You'll need a selection of magazines from which to cut out images of things which make us jealous, several large sheets of card, safety scissors and glue.

> This activity can be used to identify different kinds of jealousy.

Start by discussing the sort of things we might be jealous of; for example:

- Jealousy about things—wanting things that other people have

★ Jealousy about status—wanting to be like (or be!) other people

- Jealousy about opportunity—wanting to achieve the same status as other people

Split into small groups and ask each group to cut out as many images as possible of things that make us jealous—or have the potential to make us jealous—from the magazines, and build them into a huge collage. Mount them on the card in the shape of something which makes the group think of jealousy, for example a sports car—or even a dragon to depict the green-eyed monster!

Drama

Start by discussing how the puppet play can be broken down into scenes; for example:

1. **Darius conferring status on Daniel.**

2. **The jealousy of the advisers.**

3. **Daniel praying.**

4. **The plot of the advisers.**

5. **The advisers go to Darius.**

6. **Daniel praying.**

7. **Daniel's arrest.**

8. **Daniel's sentence.**

9. **With the lions.**

10. **Darius' anxiety.**

11. **Darius' relief.**

(You can add the little coda to the story where the advisers get eaten if you must!)

> There is a moral dimension to the fate of Daniel's accusers, who would have been perfectly aware of the possible consequences of their deceit should they be found out—yet they went ahead. Clearly they did not care for the fate of Daniel or have a concern for the danger that they were placing others in. It is worth noting that any of our actions can have consequences that we ignore or overlook—but that does not make us any the less responsible!

Now work out the script. A dramatized Bible might help with scripting, but you will still have to work on each scene to bring out the main points. The aim is to try to get closer to the story and see faith in the context of the political regime and context in which Daniel finds himself. Ask the question: 'How did Daniel maintain his faith in a strange land?' This leads on to the corollary of the faithfulness of God to Daniel, in the light of Daniel's own obedient faith.

The theatre

A two-tier puppet theatre would work very well for this play. The king performs on the top level and Daniel, with the lions, in the lower space! This allows the audience to see that Daniel is OK without the king knowing—a fairly common dramatic trick! It is no use trying to surprise the audience with

Daniel's survival: the story is too well-known.

Make the theatre from cardboard boxes or wood.

Allow the script to develop over several 'improvized' rehearsals. If you tape (or video) the rehearsals you can pick out especially good phrases and ideas to be included in the final show.

Encourage the children to see the story as individual scenes as well as the whole.

Prayers

Dear Lord,
We often find it hard to
follow you.
Help us to remember Daniel
and your faithfulness to him
when you were all that he had. Amen

Father of all,
In our world there are many who are
betrayed,
many who are imprisoned,
and many who are sentenced to death
for having faith in you.
We pray for all your people:
be with them and strengthen them
so that through all their troubles they
will feel your love
and in the end come with joy to your
kingdom,
through Jesus Christ. Amen

Drawing Together

Finding God in the darkness

This act of worship contains five readings which are designed to create an atmosphere of darkness.

Invite the children to sit in a circle. Darken the room as much as you can. Each of the first five readings is read by torchlight, after which the torch is turned off. Place several reading lamps around the room, outside of the circle. Plug them into extension cables running from one switched socket.

Reader 1 …in the darkness all the wild animals come out.
The young lions roar while they hunt…
(Psalm 104:20–21)

Reader 2 You have thrown me into the depths of the tomb,
into the darkest and deepest pit…
Are your miracles seen in that place of darkness
or your goodness in the land of the forgotten?
(Psalm 88:6 and 12)

Reader 3 You have made even my closest friends abandon me,
and darkness is my only companion.
(Psalm 88:18)

Reader 4 The star opened the abyss, and smoke poured out of it,
like the smoke from a large furnace;
the sunlight and the air were darkened by the smoke from the abyss.
(Revelation 9:2)

As soon as the final reading begins, all the lights are switched on simultaneously from the switched socket.

Reader 5 'I am the light of the world,' he said.
'Whoever follows me will have the light of life
and will never walk in darkness.'
(John 8:12)

Finish with a prayer.

Theme Extension

It is instructive to compare Daniel's experience with that of Jesus:

ⓖ **Both falsely accused for political reasons**

ⓖ **Both condemned to death**

ⓖ **Both rescued by God**

It is a theme worth pursuing with older children. You might like to research similarities between the story of Daniel in the lions' den and Jesus' trial, death and resurrection. This could lead in to a discussion on faithfulness—to what extent is this quality only worthwhile if we hold on to it through times of complete despair and hopelessness?

The Son of God

Who do you say I am?

Focus

Who is Jesus?
This question baffled many people during Jesus' lifetime and it baffles many people today. In this session we look at how Jesus dealt with some of the questions about who he was, and we examine the response of those who met God in Jesus.

> **JOHN 10:34–38**
>
> 'As for me, the Father chose me and sent me into the world.'

This is a challenging passage because it involves Jesus' use of the scriptures to defend himself and to point out the contradiction in the accusations of the people who wanted to arrest him for blasphemy. Jesus does not deny that he is the Son of God, but he points out that the scriptures refer to all God's people as sons of God.

We might feel more at home with the term 'children' of God, but the word 'son' had a special significance in Jesus' day. Sons had rights of inheritance which brought with them great responsibilities: for example, to 'defend the rights of the poor and the orphans; be fair to the needy and the helpless. Rescue them from the power of the wicked.' (Psalm 82:3–4) This psalm also makes reference to the failure of humankind to fulfil these responsibilities.

When Boot landed us in Peter's fishing boat we learnt some amazing things about Jesus.

That was on pages 24–30 of Searchlights and Secrets—it was a good job I had the torch!

Discussion Starters

Pick out the words in the passage about *why* we should believe that Jesus is the Son of God. What would make the children believe that someone was the Son of God?

How do you respond to someone who keeps on telling you that they are, say, really brilliant at netball—but never plays and won't join the school team? Would you believe them?

★ What would make you believe them?

Is it only actions that convince us?

Activities

Making triptychs— three deeds of Jesus

> This activity looks at the different miracles and teachings which are important aspects of Jesus' ministry.

> You'll need card, paper, paint, pens, pencils, scissors, glue and possibly wood and wire too.

Triptychs can easily be made of card, but you can make more substantial ones using wood, if you wish!

The idea of these is to make up three pictures showing different aspects of the work of Jesus, which lead us to the conclusion that he actually was the Son of God. A possible structure for this is to use the following:

One illustration of Jesus' teaching

★ One illustration of Jesus' miracles

One illustration of Jesus' status in God's eyes

Each child (or groups if you prefer) creates three pictures which form the triptych.

The annunciation, baptism and transfiguration of Jesus all point to the man who is God. These positive signs of the divinity of the Son of God seem to form a backdrop in the gospels to the miracles and teaching ministry, against which we see the disbelief and belief of the people that Jesus encountered, acted out as if on a stage.

You might like to use collage effects to create your pictures—the results can be very impressive. Use pieces of cloth for clothes, bits of gold and silver thread, etc. This will make each panel thicker and you must allow for this when folding card.

Make two folds at the dotted lines to allow for the thickness of the collage work.

Triptychs can be made of wood and held together with loops of wire, but this is not recommended if you are not used to making them!

Who do you say that I am?

You'll need some stiff white card, cut into 52 equally-sized rectangles to make the playing cards, pens and colouring pencils.

You'll need to make up one pack of cards for every seven players.

First, the group have to make up the pack of cards with four cards of each character or group. Write the names, what they said and the Bible reference on the cards and draw a picture of the person or group, as follows:

Disciples	Truly you are the son of God! (Matthew 14:33)
Mark	This is the Good News about Jesus Christ the Son of God. (Mark 1:1)
John	We saw his glory, the glory which he received as the Father's only son. (John 1:14)
Simeon	With my own eyes I have seen your salvation. (Luke 2:30)
Army Officer	This man was really the Son of God! (Mark 15:39)
Angel	The holy child will be called the Son of God. (Luke 1:35)
John the Baptist	I tell you that he is the Son of God. (John 1:34)
Peter	You are the Messiah. (Mark 8:29)
Pharisees	The man who did this cannot be from God, for he does not obey the Sabbath law. (John 9:16)
The people	You are only a man, but you are trying to make yourself God! (John 10:33)
Chief priests	The only king we have is the Emperor! (John 19:15)
The High Priest	You have just heard his blasphemy! (Matthew 26:65)
Soldiers	After the soldiers had crucified Jesus they took his clothes and divided them into four parts, one part for each soldier. (John 19:23)

To play the game, give each player seven cards and place the rest face-down on the table, with the top card turned face-up beside the pile.

The first player either picks up a card from the face-down pile and discards one on to the face-up pile, or asks a specific player for a specific card. If they have the card they must give it to the asker, who must give them a card in return. If the asker guesses correctly that the player has the card they requested, they get a free go, continuing until they guess incorrectly.

Play then moves to the next player on the left. If the face-down pile is used up, then the face-up pile is shuffled and turned face-down, with the top card once again placed face-up beside the pile.

The winner is the first person to collect seven of the eight characters/groups who knew that Jesus was the son of God.

You could also play 'pairs' with the cards, with the person to collect the highest number of pairs of the eight characters/groups who knew that Jesus was the Son of God being the winner.

Prayers

Father God,
Strengthen our faith
and open our eyes,
to see who Jesus really is,
and not to reject him. Amen

Dear Lord,
We have heard the stories of Jesus.
We have heard of his works.
Bring a true faith to all who hear,
Lord, we pray,
that your kingdom may come
through your son. Amen

Drawing Together

Questions and answers

This act of worship follows the lines of a question-and-answer dialogue. This form is used by the Jewish people both in worship and in teaching. It is a very ancient pattern and may well have been in common use during Jesus' lifetime. It is heavily adapted here!

All	Who was Jesus?
Reader 1	It was the will of the Lord that his servant should grow like a plant.
Reader 2	He had no dignity or beauty to make us take notice of him.
All	Who was Jesus?
Reader 1	We despised him and rejected him; he endured suffering and pain.
Reader 2	No one would even look at him—we ignored him as if he were nothing.
All	Who was Jesus?
Reader 1	Because of our sins he was wounded.
Reader 2	Beaten because of the evil we did.
All	Who was Jesus?
Reader 1	He was arrested and sentenced and led off to die.
Reader 2	He was put to death for the sins of our people.
All	Who was Jesus?
Reader 1	I will give him a place of honour.
Reader 2	A place among the great and powerful.
All	Who is Jesus?
Reader 3	Jesus Christ is Lord, to the glory of God the Father.
All	Who is Jesus?
Readers	He is the visible likeness of the invisible God.

Finish with a prayer or grace.

Weakness and strength

Focus

Where does our strength come from? This session aims to take a practical look at this question. We need to see our strength as something that is completely underpinned by the sustenance of God. Food, drink and exercise are, of course, essential to our well-being, but in fact these things are still reliant upon God's providence.

We learnt about the Holy Spirit on pages 53–59 of *Tiptoes and Fingertips*.

Scene Setter

ACTS 2:1–6

...they saw what looked like tongues of fire which spread out and touched each person there.

In this passage we find the disciples being anointed with the Holy Spirit and thereby given the strength to begin their work. This story must be seen in the context of the instructions from Jesus that they were to wait for the gift of the Holy Spirit. Their strength was to be from God and without God's strength the mission to which they were called would have been far less likely to succeed. The coming of the Holy Spirit upon the disciples in many ways endorses the teaching of Jesus as the good shepherd. Just as the sheep must rely on their shepherd to guide them, so we, as the body of Christ, are called to follow Christ in the strength of his Spirit.

Discussion Starters

Explore ways in which we can draw closer to God: for example, by reading his word in the Bible, by singing his praise, or through prayer.

★ **What role does the Holy Spirit play in our being close to God?**

★ **In what situations do we feel that the Holy Spirit makes a difference?**

★ **In what situations do we find it hard to feel close to God?**

★ **What could we do to change that?**

★ **What did Jesus promise?**

Activities

The Holy Spirit gives us strength

This is a messy but effective illustration of our need for God's Spirit!

You will need a packet of spaghetti and some weights ranging from one gram upwards—a school might be able to lend you these.

Start by suspending the smallest weight from one strand of spaghetti. How much weight will the strand carry before breaking? Now try two strands and so on. You will find that the spaghetti becomes quite strong with surprisingly few strands. The problem is in keeping the strands together—try using rubber bands, thread or sticky tape.

Point out that when we work together, bound together by the Holy Spirit of God, we can do much more than we can on our own.

Discuss this and encourage the group to see that we need to be held together if we are to be strong, to carry the weights that God asks us to.

- 🌀 **Discuss what the 'weights' might be: sharing, prayer...**

- 🌀 **Discuss what the 'binding' might be: the Holy Spirit, bread and wine...**

Next you will need several newspapers or sheets of card, some strips of plain paper, sticky tape, pens, a basket, some small boxes and brown paper.

Now make a display to illustrate how we carry the weight of the work that God asks us to do together. Roll up several newspapers or sheets of card. Cut some strips of paper and write the 'binding' words on them, for example, the Holy Spirit or bread and wine. Bind the rolls with the paper strips and suspend a basket from them. Make some parcels from small boxes covered with brown paper and label them with the weights, for example, sharing, prayer... Put the parcels into the basket.

What other 'binding' things can you think of?

We thought of some great 'weights'. What can you think of?

God is with us in our weakness

You will need large sheets of paper or some lining wallpaper, old magazines and glue.

Explore and discuss some of the ways in which people are weakened.

- ★ **Through poverty...**

- ★ **Through hunger...**

- ★ **As a result of war...**

- ★ **Through illness...**

Lead this into a discussion about how God is present in suffering and brings strength and courage in these situations.

From the magazines and newspapers, make up a collective collage depicting some of the things you have been discussing. Lay the collage out in the shape of a cross and use it as a focus for drawing together in worship.

Music and Dance

The coming of the Spirit

The passage from Acts 2 can be interpreted through dance. You need contrasting music for the first part where the disciples are afraid and for the second part when they are filled with the Holy Spirit and begin to speak in tongues.

In designing this dance you will have to decide whether to begin with the music or the movement. The outline of the dance is as follows:

1. **The disciples gather together, afraid.**

2. **The disciples share bread and wine.**

3. **The sound of the Spirit is heard; this grows louder.**

4. **Flames begin to appear.**

5. **The noise reaches its peak and there are many flames.**

6. The disciples begin to spread the good news as the flames die away.

This is the basic outline, but you can add the crowd gathering around the disciples if you have enough people to do it. The 'flames' are most effective in costume—they could simply wear red clothes (but try not to have football team logos on the clothes, as this will spoil the effect!) The flames begin by simply weaving singly through the disciples and disappearing. They gradually increase in number; it is very effective if the number of flames match the number of disciples, as they can then stand briefly behind each one before departing as the disciples go out to spread the good news.

Make your own music for this. You will need to decide on both the sound and the rhythm. The gathering of the disciples needs to be hesitant. The flames begin quietly, but need a quick, distinctive rhythm of their own (a folk-style 6/8 beat is effective). The end needs to be decisive and strong. If you feel confident enough you could explore appropriate melodies. You could write your own, or use hymn or dance tunes. Try slowing them down or speeding them up, or repeating a short section using different instruments when the flames come on.

We had great fun experimenting with this!

Prayers

Almighty God,
You are our strength.
You are the strength we bring to others
when we help them in your name.
Bind us with your Holy Spirit so that we,
like the first apostles before us,
may be strong to do your work.
In Jesus' name. **Amen**

Father God,
We are weak
when we are sad, alone, or hurting.
We need your strength
to find your joy, your church and your healing.
Thank you that you give this strength
and thank you that you are with us in our weakness.
Through your son, Jesus Christ. **Amen**

Holy God,
Send us your Spirit
so that we can always
walk in your strength
and need never fear
those things that
threaten to overwhelm us. **Amen**

Drawing Together

You will need a selection of things that help to make us strong. For example, breakfast cereals, lightweight exercise equipment (weights etc.), milk , fresh fruit and vegetables.

Lay the collage you made earlier on a table at the front of the room and set out the items on top of it.

Reader 1 *Read Psalm 23*

Reader 2 Thank you, heavenly Father, that you provide these things to make us strong.

Reader 3 Thank you for the things that give us your strength.

Child The strength of your word.
(*Places a Bible on the table.*)

Child The strength of your cross.
(*Places a cross on the table.*)

Child The strength of your body.
(*Places bread on the table.*)

Child The strength of your life.
(*Places wine on the table.*)

Child The strength of your light in the world.
(*Places a candle on the table.*)

Reader 1 *Read Psalm 23 again.*

Theme Extension

You could use this session to develop ideas of what we mean by strength. One of the strongest images in the twentieth century has been the sharing of weakness to create a position of strength, for example, with Gandhi, Tutu and Mandela. There are also examples of people, such as Mother Teresa, who have given strength to many through their weakness. Develop the discussion by encouraging children to think about the difference between strength and force. How do individuals, such as dictators, wield their force?

Paul's journeys (1)

Focus

Paul's journeys represent not so much the beginning of the Church as the beginning of the mission to the gentiles. Many Christians have made a great deal out of Paul's role as the leading evangelist of the early church. But, whilst we mustn't diminish the significance of Paul's work, we need to remember that he was one of a large group of people working right across the eastern Mediterranean, bringing Christian witness to a great many people. Paul himself indicates this in his letters. There *are* other letters in the New Testament besides those of Paul and, of course, Acts records the activity of several of the apostles. This needs to be borne in mind when we work with the material, so that we can convey the full breadth of the New Testament picture of early evangelism.

> **Boot took us travelling with Paul in Trackers and Trainers.**

> **It all started when I escaped into Timothy's garden on page 40.**

Scene Setter

> **ACTS 13:1–3, 13–33A AND 42–52**
>
> **While they were serving the Lord and fasting, the Holy Spirit said to them, 'Set apart for me Barnabas and Saul, to do the work to which I have called them.'**

This is a long passage, covering most of Acts 13, and it is important to read the passage through several times to familiarize yourself with the context of Paul's preaching ministry. Once you have done so, summarize the text for your group, making sure you include the following important points:

1. The initial commissioning of Paul and his companions was carried out in obedience to the direction of the Holy Spirit.

2. This is the first time that the Roman version of Paul's name is used.

3. Paul's sermon is set within the Jewish synagogue, thus making the content of his preaching, based on the Jewish Scriptures, highly significant.

4. The jealousy of the Jewish people leads to Paul's mission to the gentiles and ultimately to the Jewish persecution of Paul.

Discussion Starters

Begin by discussing together what it feels like to be chosen. What is it like to be chosen for a team, for a play, to do a job…?

The task that Paul was chosen to do required a lot of travelling. If possible, show a map of the eastern Mediterranean to demonstrate the scale of Paul's journeys.

🌀 **What might be a similar example of Paul's mission today?**

★ **Who would you want to travel with you if you were to go on such a journey?**

Activities

Travelling with Paul

> **You will need a selection of travel books, a map, scissors, glue, pens and paper.**

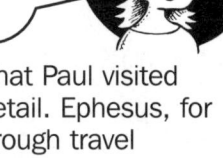

Choose one or two of the places that Paul visited on his travels to look at in more detail. Ephesus, for example, can be brought to life through travel brochures and books.

Discuss such things as the sorts of buildings he might have seen and the type of houses he might have stayed in. If anyone in your group has been to the place you choose, ask them to bring in photographs or souvenirs.

Investigate the kind of boat that Paul would have used and discuss why he travelled by sea so much. A map of the Mediterranean can be used to show that many of the places he visited were by the coast. The sea was the highway of Paul's day. Land travel would have been difficult and time-consuming.

Put together a display of 'Paul's world' with a map of the area showing just a few of the places he visited, together with pictures from brochures, photographs, souvenirs and the children's own drawings of the places.

Bible detectives

Notice that Luke's name appears in Colossians 4:14, but is not mentioned in the book of Acts.

The children might like to do a bit of detective work on this.

First of all, ask the children to look at the beginning of Luke's Gospel and the beginning of Acts. This will give them their first clue: Acts is a second book written for Theophilus.

Secondly, if Luke is the author of the gospel attributed to him, then it seems that the book of Acts was also written by Luke. (This is *not* certain, of course, but the evidence is rather overwhelming!)

Finally, look at Acts 16:1–15. Notice the changes from 'they' to 'we' and 'us'. Why does this happen? This is the third clue: it must be because Luke was there and therefore includes himself in the text at the point when he starts travelling with the others.

Games

Where did Paul go? Whom did he meet? A board game

You will need a large sheet of paper, a protractor, pencils and coloured pens, stiff card, a dice and 24 counters.

You will have to find out some of the people that Paul travelled with. Here are some to start you off:

Acts 13: 4 and 5	Barnabas and John Mark
Acts 15:40	Silas
Acts 16:1 and 2	Timothy
Acts 19:22	Erastus

These are all from the book of Acts, which records the things that Paul did. The following are from Paul's own letters.

Romans 16:1–16	Phoebe, Priscilla, Aquila, Urbanus
Colossians 4:10–14	Aristarchus, Joshua, Epaphras and Luke. (Mark and Barnabas get in here too!)
Titus 3:12	Artemas and Tychicus (well, we couldn't miss this one, could we?)

You need 16 people in all. The game is made like this...

⊚ **Draw two concentric circles and divide them into 18 segments each of 20 degrees (use a protractor).**

★ **Choose one of the segments to be the start, and one to its left to be the end. In each of the remaining segments draw one of the characters that Paul met. You can choose different ones to those above, of course.**

⊚ **Make a set of cards, each with one of the characters on it.**

★ **You will also need a dice and 24 counters or coloured card discs.**

The game is played like this:

Each player is dealt four cards and is given six counters. The first player 'puts in' some counters, the others then do the same but cannot put the same number as the player whose turn it is. The player then rolls the dice. If the dice matches the number of counters that the player put in, then they can move any number of spaces *up to* the number on the dice. If it does not match, but matches the number of counters *another* player has put in, then that player *must* move the whole number on the dice. Players can move either way round the circle but cannot change direction during one turn.

The object of the game is to land on the squares of the characters on the cards you are holding. When you do so, you give up the card. Once you have given up all four cards, a player moves to the Finish segment. You need not score the exact number needed to finish, but you cannot land on the Finish square until you have given up all your cards.

As with all games, it is much harder to explain than to play—try it, it's fun, and exasperating. (A bit like sailing around the Mediterranean islands!)

Drama

One of the recurrent themes in Paul's work was his preaching. Not many of Paul's sermons are recorded in the book of Acts, but Paul's speech to the Athenians in Acts 17:22–31 forms the core of his message. This passage shows us that the central point of Paul's preaching was about Jesus. What would the group say about Jesus if they were given the chance?

Split the group into smaller groups of three or four and ask them to write a 'sermon' based on Paul's speech to the Athenians. What do they think are the most important points? Which verses would they want to stress most? Why?

This exercise could provide an opportunity to listen to some modern day preaching. If you meet during a service you could arrange to go into church and listen to the sermon, then go out and talk about what you heard. How close was it to what Paul was preaching? If it was very different, why was it very different?

Prayers

Father God,
In our prayers we remember
all those people who have
brought your good news to new places
and shared the stories of your son
Jesus Christ.
Thank you for their work and witness.
Amen

Lord,
We pray for all those who are working
to make your name known in the world today.
Some are preaching your word.
Some are bringing your healing touch.
Some are praying.
Some are writing.
Others are working unnoticed by all but you.
Be with them in their work, we pray.
In Jesus' name. Amen

Drawing Together

Begin the act of worship by reading the story of Paul and Silas in prison.

ACTS 16:16–40

You might like to use a children's Bible for this, or write the story in your own words together as a group.

Then, like Paul and Silas, sing some hymns, or songs that you know well. Have a really good sing-song. End by briefly mentioning the need for Christians to stay 'in touch' with God, through singing and prayer. End with a prayer.

Theme Extension

The study of Paul's mission raises the issue of conversion and, with a little biblical research, this can make an interesting discussion.

⊚ **What do we mean by 'conversion'?**

★ **What were the people to whom Paul brought the gospel turning to and from?**

⊚ **In what ways is this the same today?**

★ **In what ways does it differ?**

⊚ **What other religions were prevalent in Paul's day?**

★ **How did Paul take his message to people of different cultures and religions?**

⊚ **Is there an example for us to follow today in the way Paul worked?**

Calendar Link

Trinity—the spreading church through the work of the Holy Spirit

Trinity begins with Pentecost—the coming of the Spirit—and runs right through to Advent.

It is a very useful exercise to look through the book of Acts, which tells of the beginnings of the church, to see how often the Holy Spirit is mentioned. We tend to think of the book of Acts as being about Paul and the other apostles—after doing this, you might change your mind!

Paul's journeys (2)

Focus

This session focuses on the establishment of the early church. Paul is often seen as simply a fearless preacher and worker of miracles. Whilst this image carries some truth, it misses the mark by a long way. Paul, as his letters show, was concerned for the whole Christian life, and the whirlwind accounts of his journeys need to be held in balance with the more reflective comments in his letters.

Following Paul was great—until I discovered I couldn't swim!

That was on page 59 of Trackers and Trainers—Tychi came to the rescue!

Scene Setter

ACTS 19:8–10

Paul went into the synagogue and during three months spoke boldly with the people.

This short passage emphasizes the fact that Paul did not simply hop from place to place, but spent time establishing relationships. This leads on to the discussion points which concern keeping in touch, which Paul did through his letters, of course.

Discussion Starters

Discuss different ways of keeping in contact, and why we might want to stay in contact with people.

- **Who do we know from different parts of the world?**

- **How do we keep in contact?**

- **Why might Paul have wanted to stay in contact with the churches that he helped to begin?**

Activities

Keeping in contact with God through prayer

We wrote our own prayers, based on the prayers of Paul.

And then we prayed them together!

You'll need paper and pens or pencils for everyone in the group.

This activity aims to show how prayers have been built up from different parts of the Bible. Most of us know that the Lord's Prayer is in the Bible, but we might not realize that the words of the Grace, for example, also come from the Bible.

Read out the following passages:

- ★ **Romans 16:25–27**

- ★ **2 Corinthians 1:3–5 and 13:3**

- ★ **Ephesians 1:3–14 and 23–24**

Next invite the group to write their own prayers based on these passages. The passages may not all be 'prayers' in the exact sense, but they are all 'prayerful' and give us a good basis for the kinds of things that believers have used in prayers for 2000 years. When we say or write prayers, our thoughts and voices join with those who have prayed down the years.

Paul also gives us guidance about *how* to pray. In the busyness of his travelling ministry he remembers to pray for all those he has worked with, all the churches he has established and those who belong to them. Read out the following passage as an example of this fact:

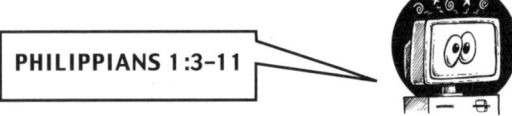

PHILIPPIANS 1:3–11

This is not just an interesting point to notice, it is critical to the whole of Paul's ministry. Faith, work and prayer are all linked together in Paul's life in the same way that they were linked in the ministry of Jesus. If we are to be part of the kingdom that Paul travelled so far to tell people about, we too must have faith, work hard and pray hard.

It is important to understand this, but it should be seen not as a duty of moral obedience, but as a response to the love of God. This is the essence of Paul's prayer in Philippians.

Keeping in contact with God through symbols

Many people keep images and symbols to remind them of the places they have been, or friends who live far away. Christians through the ages have built up many symbols and images which keep them in contact with God in the same way that pictures or objects keep us in contact with friends or family. There are biblical symbols such as fire, light or the dove and other 'church' or community symbols such as the ICHTHUS fish which came to be of some importance in the early church.

Discuss the different symbols we use as Christians. In particular talk through the distinctions between 'sacramental' symbols, such as bread and wine or water, which play a role in our church worship and other symbols, such as the fish or dove.

The ICHTHUS fish is a tremendous symbol. Not only did it serve as a sign of recognition for Christians, especially those hiding from persecution, but it is also a mini 'creed'.

On page 45 in Footsteps and Fingerprints, we found out what ICHTHUS stands for.

'Jesus Christ, God's Son, Saviour' is a statement of Christian belief about Jesus. The same is true of the various crosses that we see, an empty cross indicating a belief in the resurrection, a crucifix indicating a belief in Christ truly dying for us, etc. Paul was as concerned about stating right belief about Jesus and God as we are today. Read Colossians 1:15–20 with the children, and talk about the kinds of things that we believe as Christians.

The group can then think of symbols of their own to show an aspect of Christian faith which they think is important. Allow them lots of freedom in doing this. Their ideas may well be expressed in naive or unconventional ways, but it is important to encourage each child to develop their understanding in the context of their Christian faith and sense of belonging to the family of God.

Dance

A very powerful dance can be created using Colossians 1:15–20, making a series of movements around a central figure who represents Jesus.

This dance is very effective if done well.

Reader

Christ is the visible likeness of the invisible God. He is the firstborn Son, superior to all created things.

The dancer representing Jesus is raised and brought to the centre by the other dancers.

Reader

For through him God created everything in heaven and on earth, the seen and the unseen things...

The dancers circle around the central figure, crouching, rising and falling, as if they were waves.

Reader

...including the spiritual powers, lords, rulers and authorities.

As each is mentioned, one or more dancers stop and face the central figure until all are perfectly still, they remain still for the next line.

Reader

God created the whole universe through him and for him.

Pause

Reader

Christ existed before all things...

The dancers extend their arms and reach out as if pointing to all the things around the room, world etc.

Reader

...and in union with him all things have their proper place.

The dancers link hands with each others to form a web around the central figure.

Reader

He is the head of his body, the church; he is the source of the body's life.

The dancers move to kneel before the central figure. They then slowly turn and begin to crawl away from the central figure, who sinks to the floor and curls into a ball.

Reader

He is the firstborn Son, who was raised from death, in order that he alone might have first place in all things. For it was by God's own decision that the Son has in himself the full nature of God.

The dancers continue to move away and the central figure kneels up at the word 'death'.

Reader

Through the Son, then, God decided to bring the whole universe back to himself.

The dancers still move slowly away whilst the central figure stands and reaches out, steadily opening his or her arms wider as the reader continues. When the word 'cross' is reached, the central figure should have his/her arms stretched right out in a cross shape.

Reader

God made peace through his Son's sacrificial death on the cross...

The dancers stop and turn toward the central figure.

Reader

...and so brought back to himself all things, both on earth and in heaven.

The dancers very slowly move toward the central figure, finally surrounding him/her as in an embrace. The dancers freeze their position whilst the central figure slowly lowers his/her arms to embrace them.

These movements are only suggestions and you might wish to alter them. The variant reading 'sacrificial death' has been used deliberately to emphasize the purpose of Jesus' act. The dance can be performed with just the readings and movement or over a backdrop of music such as Tavener's 'Akathist of Thanksgiving', or soft guitar music. This can be enhanced with sound-effects, with the children using percussion instruments to indicate footsteps, hammer blows etc.

Drawing Together

This act of worship is a simple drawing together in prayer. Children can sometimes find it difficult to concentrate during times of prayer. Try using something for them to focus on, such as their own symbols or a lighted candle. If you want to encourage 'open prayer' remember that not everyone will want to join in. Make sure that everyone knows that they do not have to pray aloud if they do not wish to do so. You can use the prayers written during the activity or simply use some of the prayers from Paul's letters.

Theme Extension

You might like to write letters to a young people's/children's group at another church, just as Paul wrote to churches. This could become a regular point of contact with another group. This could be extended to establish a relationship with a church somewhere else in the world, particularly if your church has missionary links. Speak to your minister about it if you think that it might be a good idea.

Commitment

Focus

This session picks out family commitments as an example of what it means to be committed. The concept of a committed family is based on the tableau painted of the family at Bethany.

We met Martha and Mary in Families and Feelings on pages 46–52.

Scene Setter

JOHN 11:1–44

'Didn't I tell you that you would see God's glory if you believed?'

The story of the raising of Lazarus needs to be told in its entirety to include the dialogue between Jesus and the disciples as well as the response of the people.

Much has been surmised as to why Jesus waited for two days before going to see Lazarus. He seems to have waited deliberately until Lazarus died, and the text seems to suggest that Jesus was working in God's own way for the greater good. Yet Jesus seems also to have put himself through a great deal of emotional pain in the unfolding of this story.

Discussion Starters

Begin by focusing on Mary and Martha. Did their commitment to Jesus waver in the face of this tragedy? Are Mary's words in verse 32 a criticism of Jesus or simply an observation that Jesus had great power? Let the group talk this through and then lead on to discuss the following points:

🔘 **What does it mean to be committed to each other?**

🔘 **What does it mean to be committed to a faith or a cause?**

🔘 **To which of the following was Jesus showing commitment?**

  1. God?
  2. Lazarus?
  3. Mary and Martha?
  4. His disciples?
  5. The law?

Discussion Extension

In the story of the boy Jesus in the temple from Luke 2:41–52, we find a powerful commitment to the 'Father' in Jesus, but no diminishing of his commitment to his family, as the last few verses of the chapter indicate. This passage provides the basis for a discussion on the way that we resolve our own clashes of commitment to family, clubs, church etc.

Activities

Keeping in touch

You will need paper, scissors, glue, coloured paper, pens and paints.

Cards are an expression of our commitment. We choose them carefully to convey our feelings to the recipient.

First of all, discuss together the type of card which we might send to the following people:

★ **A thank you card for a relative**

★ **A birthday card for a friend**

★ **A get well card for a neighbour**

★ **A card replying to an invitation**

Next, discuss the type of design that would be appropriate. The design shows something of the relationship you have with a person. If you know, for example, that a person likes boats you might design a card with a boat on it. If you know someone's favourite colour you might make a card with an abstract design in shades of that colour.

Cards indicate other significant factors—something shared (sympathy cards), something special (birthday cards)—or can be given as gifts (special pictures). You might be able to think of more than this.

What sort of card might we send to God to show our relationship to him?

Invite each member of the group to design a card that they would like to send to God. First they will need to draw out their design and then decide on the method of decorating it. Rather than simply colouring the design, they might like to try torn paper collage. To do this you simply need lots of bits of different coloured paper. Striking effects can be achieved by using different colours and/or different kinds of paper. For example, blotting paper tears differently from brown paper.

Note that the rainbow in Genesis 9:12–16 is a sign to God about the promise—it still reminds us, though!

Use these examples of signs for God's promises:

★ **Genesis 9:13**

★ **Genesis 21:1**

★ **Deuteronomy 1:11**

★ **2 Samuel 7:28–29**

Try looking in the letter to the Hebrews for some more references to promises. Choose appropriate media for the symbols, from simple drawing through collage to sculpture and appliqué—be as imaginative as you like.

Signs of a promise

You'll need to decide beforehand what media you want to use; you'll probably want paper, pencils, paint, glue, scissors and sticky tape, whichever you choose!

Promises are commitments. We have many signs to remind us that promises have been made, for example, money, contracts, wedding rings and our signatures.

Start by discussing the different signs of commitment. Then move on to signs of promise from God: the rainbow, the law, the cross... you might like to introduce other ideas such as the tassels on the Jewish tallith (prayer shawl) being reminders of the Law.

Games

This is a chance to play some team games.

If you have the space, games like crab football or benchball bring out the commitment theme very well.

Crab football needs only a fairly large space, a ball and a way of indicating goals. Don't have teams of more than five. Each player, except the goalie who kneels, has to move crab-fashion, but face up, with arms and legs behind them. The idea is to score (of course!). Play for a limited time, say three minutes each way, and see who scores the most goals. Remember that this is *football* so the ball must be kicked. Only the goalie can use hands. Oh, and goalies can throw, but cannot score!

Benchball needs two benches and a ball. The benches must be strong and stable, as the players will need to stand on them.

Draw an area across the middle of the playing area with chalk, like this...

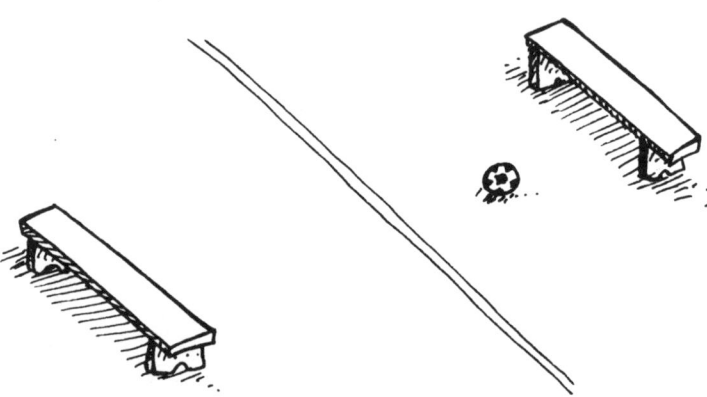

Prayers

Father God,
We know that you love us;
you have shown this through the ages
in the lives of Noah, Abraham, Moses,
David and Daniel.
You have shown us all your love
in the life of Jesus.
Be with us as we remember your
commitment to us
and help us to remember our
commitment to you.
In Jesus' name. **Amen**

Dear Lord,
As we pray
we remember when you walked on
this earth:
the people you met
and whose lives you touched.
In all that we do for you throughout
our lives,
help us to remember your commitment
to the world that you saved
and save again each day. **Amen**

The players then roll the ball to try to hit the opponents below the knee. If a player is struck below the knee by the ball, even accidentally, they become a captive and have to go round the side of the court and stand on the bench in the opposing area. They can escape by catching the ball either from a direct throw from their own side, or from a bounce. They then return to their own side of the court with the ball. The game can be played either until all of a team have been 'captured', or for a set time after which the team with the most captives wins. This number does not include any captives who have escaped. This game can be made more exciting by using more than one ball!

Drawing Together

This act of worship takes the form of an 'antiphonal' psalm, using an adapted version of Psalm 136.

Use one of the prayers before and after this piece. You could add a song too if you wish.

Reader
Give thanks to the Lord, because he is good.

All   God's love is eternal.

Reader
Give thanks to the greatest of all.

All   God's love is eternal.

Reader
Give thanks to the mightiest of all lords.

All   God's love is eternal.

Reader
Only God performs great miracles.

All   God's love is eternal.

Reader
By the Lord's wisdom the heavens were made.

All   God's love is eternal.

Reader
God built the earth on the deep waters.

All   God's love is eternal.

Reader
And made the sun and moon.

All   God's love is eternal.

Reader
God led the people of Israel out of Egypt.

All   God's love is eternal.

Reader
Divided the Red Sea.

All   God's love is eternal.

Reader
And led the people through it.

All   God's love is eternal.

Reader
He gave lands to the people.

All   God's love is eternal.

Reader
And did not forget when we were defeated.

All   God's love is eternal.

Reader
He remembered his promise to us all.

All   God's love is eternal.

Reader
And sent his Son, a light to all peoples.

All   God's love is eternal.

Reader
He freed us.

All   God's love is eternal.

Reader
Give thanks to the God of heaven.

All   God's love is eternal.

Looking after God's world

Focus

This is a very fitting summer theme to end on. There is reference to ecology and conservation in this session, but in the context of its expression as a response to God's provision in terms of good stewardship of the things that have been given to us. It is important for us to grasp the fact that things are not owned by us, but only held in trust. This is not an easy thing to learn in a society that places great value on the accumulation of material wealth. This session focuses on God as the only true creator.

Scene Setter

PSALM 148

Praise the Lord!

This is a psalm in praise of creation. We met David and heard him singing in praise of God on pages 5–6 of Tiptoes and Fingertips.

Psalm 148 is a very powerful psalm of praise to the creator. You might like to recap on the creation story before going on to the activities. The psalm is written in the context of a people who saw their origins in the work of the all-powerful creator God. This psalm does not simply indicate that *God* is great, but that *our* God is great.

Discussion Starters

Begin the discussion with the idea of looking after things. We all have valuable things that we want to protect.

Ⓖ **What do we have to look after?**

★ **Why look after it?**

★ Lead this on to thinking about other people's things.

Ⓖ **Do we take as much care over things that people lend to us as we do of our own things? Pencils, rulers, footballs etc.**

Activities

Going for a walk

You'll probably want to take paper, pencils, rubbers and so on. You may wish to take a camera or even a video with you. Don't get lost!

Don't forget to refer to the safety guidelines in the Introduction!

Go for a walk in any suitable outdoor location; for example, a wood or a park. You could make this into an opportunity to have a picnic.

Before you go, give the children these two questions to think about during the walk:

★ **What do I like or dislike about this location?**

Ⓖ **Would God agree with me?**

When you get to your meeting place, look around carefully and draw attention to details such as patterns in tree bark or types of brickwork.

Each person then draws two pictures, one of something that they liked about the location you visited, and one of something that they disliked.

If you are able to go to a country area or park, then the children might like to make collections of things. Don't let them pick flowers though—unless they are your flowers!

When you get back, discuss with the children what you have seen and go back to the questions. The things they find might fall into one of these categories:

★ **Things that some like and others don't, but agree that this is just preference: for example, the colour of a flower.**

◎ **Things that are universally appreciated: for example, a playground.**

★ **Things that are not acceptable: for example, litter.**

◎ **Things about which the children have no opinion: for example, a footpath.**

The children can make up their own 'Book of our World' in which they put their drawings. The activity can be developed by adding written work, poetry, photography etc.

A good way to remember a walk like this is to take a video camera with you. The tape can be played back as soon as you return or at a later session, if you wish. You'll need to provide a television set to watch it on—don't have the children all trying to see down the eyepiece!

Putting it into practice

You will need to collect together a selection of advertisements from magazines and newspapers.

Children are introduced to issues of recycling and conservation at school. How do they see this in the context of Christian faith?

Talk together about recycling, conservation and ecology. Allow the discussion quite a free rein, but bring it back to how these issues relate to Christian faith. What, for example, do you think God feels about recycling, about organic farming, or ecology?

There are no easy answers as to whether, for example, free-range chickens are closer to the ideal of God's kingdom than battery ones, but the group should be allowed to explore the issues. This raises the matter of our role in the world as stewards rather than masters; we are not in control.

Give the group a range of food advertisements and ask them to find images which they feel go well with our stewardship of God's earth and those which seem to show that we have tried to become the controllers. Display the two collections.

Music

To reinforce the idea of looking after a creation, why not create some music to go with the following adaptation of Psalm 148. You could try writing a tune for it, or use the tune given on page 125 and add your own accompaniments. Feel free to change the accompaniment if that suits you.

Praise the Lord from heaven
Praise with angels in the heights
Praise God, sun and moon
Praise with stars in jewelled flights

Let them all praise the Lord
By him they were made
Let them all praise the Lord
His commanding voice obeyed

Praise the Lord from the earth
Praise with monsters in the seas
Praise God, snow and hail
Praise with mountains, hills and trees
Praise God, old and young
Praise with creatures, birds and bees

Let us all praise the Lord
All the people praise
Let us all praise the Lord
All the people praise

Writing tunes is not too hard. Get the children to pick out the rhythm of the words and then clap it. (Don't worry if their rhythm is different from the one in the printed tune—it may be much better!) Move on to encouraging them to use a keyboard or other instruments to make a tune by playing different pitches. If you have no experience of music, suggest the children use *only* the black keys on a keyboard—it will then be impossible for them to get 'out of key'! You can experiment with the record facility of a keyboard, though traditional musical notation is still the best way to preserve your work.

Adding chords is more difficult, but there may well be musicians in your church who can do this for you. However, don't forget that a tune simply sung on its own can be very beautiful, so don't be afraid to just sing the melody.

CLAPPIT'S COFFEE

IT'S CHEAP! IT COSTS MUCH LESS THAN ANYONE ELSE'S COFFEE! BUY SOME TODAY!

CLAP COFF

ALL OF OUR BEANS ARE ORGANICALLY GROWN.

BAKER'S BEANS BAKER

Prayers

Creator God,
You made this world and
all that is in it.
Be with us as we live in your world
and guide us to care for it
as we would care for our own things.
Amen

Dear Lord,
Thank you for the world you have made.
We are sorry for the things that spoil it.
Help us to work together to try to
look after it in the way that pleases
you. Amen

Praise the Lord!
Praise the Lord from heaven.
He made the world and all that is in it.
All of us on the earth join
in the praise of our Lord,
for he has given us great things.
His world...
His love...
His Son...
Praise the Lord! Amen

Drawing Together

**For this act of worship you will
need a map of the world and a
collection of litter—it doesn't
have to be genuine, you can just
use food labels, small packaging
etc. (Try to get a wide variety.)**

**Use a map which doesn't matter
if it gets spoiled!**

Put the map up where it can be
seen by everyone. It *must* have a
firm back so that the litter can be
stuck on to it easily using a stick
glue, or sticky tape.

You might wish to play some
music or sing some songs
throughout the worship. This would
be particularly appropriate as the
litter is being stuck on to the map.

Leader
This is God's world from which we receive much.

All
God is the one who made the mountains
and created the winds.
He makes his thoughts known to people.
He changes day into night.
He walks on the heights of the earth.
This is his name: the Lord God Almighty!

Leader
We pray for those who tend and make our food.

*Children come forward and stick food labels or
packaging on to the map, with each label in the
appropriate place (fish labels in the sea etc...).*

Leader
We pray for those who bring us tools and
technolog.y

*Children come forward and stick technology labels
or packaging on to the map. Don't worry too much
about them being on the right countries—the idea
is that we see the world as a whole.*

Leader
We pray for those who care for us.

*The children bring labels or packaging from medicines
or sticking plaster, maybe even a plaster itself!*

Leader
We pray for the whole world and the goodness it
provides.

*Children bring any other labels. The map should be
more or less covered by now, try to leave some
indication that it is a map of the world.*

All
Your world, O God, is only ours for a while.
We pray that you will be with us as we use
its riches
and will guide us as we seek to care for
your world
and all those who live in it.
Amen

Theme Extension

You may be interested to find out more about local conservation strategies, such as Agenda 21. There may be local groups who would be willing to send out someone to talk about their work and about how you could be involved. Speak to your minister first about this. Similarly, you could act as collectors for such things as cans and bottles. You might like to suggest that the church buy a can crusher. Check locally that this is appropriate, however, as recycling is not always possible. What other ways can you think of in which your group could contribute to conservation? There may be people in your congregation or area who have some responsibility in the areas of conservation or caring; if there are, talk to them about how this work could best be approached.

Crack and Gleam

gathering conkers - a dance

Praise

Robin Sharples 1997

Look out for more Bible Adventures with
LIVEWIRES

Footsteps and Fingerprints

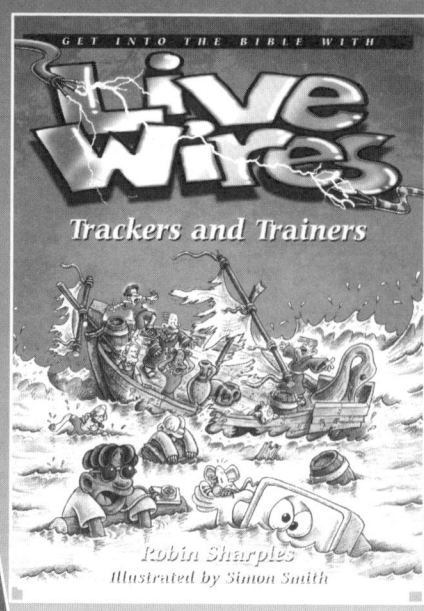

Families and Feelings

Tiptoes and Fingertips

Friends and Followers

Trackers and Trainers

Searchlights and Secrets

Special Offers!

Place your order with your local bookseller, or send your order to BRF, using the vouchers below to obtain discounted prices for bulk quantities of Livewires titles.

Footsteps and Fingerprints

Special Offer – 10 copies for only £30.00
(normal price £35.00)

SAVE £5.00

Please ensure you complete the reverse side of this voucher.
Note to booksellers: Please post this voucher with your order.
Books will be invoiced (firm sale only) at the special offer price less normal trade terms.

LL0398

Families and Feelings

Special Offer – 10 copies for only £30.00
(normal price £35.00)

SAVE £5.00

Please ensure you complete the reverse side of this voucher.
Note to booksellers: Please post this voucher with your order.
Books will be invoiced (firm sale only) at the special offer price less normal trade terms.

LL0398

Friends and Followers

Special Offer – 10 copies for only £30.00
(normal price £35.00)

SAVE £5.00

Please ensure you complete the reverse side of this voucher.
Note to booksellers: Please post this voucher with your order.
Books will be invoiced (firm sale only) at the special offer price less normal trade terms.

LL0398

Tiptoes and Fingertips

Special Offer – 10 copies for only £30.00
(normal price £35.00)

SAVE £5.00

Please ensure you complete the reverse side of this voucher.
Note to booksellers: Please post this voucher with your order.
Books will be invoiced (firm sale only) at the special offer price less normal trade terms.

LL0398

Trackers and Trainers

Special Offer – 10 copies for only £30.00
(normal price £35.00)

SAVE £5.00

Please ensure you complete the reverse side of this voucher.
Note to booksellers: Please post this voucher with your order.
Books will be invoiced (firm sale only) at the special offer price less normal trade terms.

LL0398

Searchlights and Secrets

Special Offer – 10 copies for only £30.00
(normal price £35.00)

SAVE £5.00

Please ensure you complete the reverse side of this voucher.
Note to booksellers: Please post this voucher with your order.
Books will be invoiced (firm sale only) at the special offer price less normal trade terms.

LL0398

Livewires Get into the Bible

Special Offer – 10 copies for only £35.00
(normal price £39.99)

SAVE £4.99

Please ensure you complete the reverse side of this voucher.
Note to booksellers: Please post this voucher with your order.
Books will be invoiced (firm sale only) at the special offer price less normal trade terms.

LL0398

Set of all 7 titles

Special Offer – whole set for only £20.00
(normal price £24.99)

SAVE £4.99

Please ensure you complete the reverse side of this voucher.
Note to booksellers: Please post this voucher with your order.
Books will be invoiced (firm sale only) at the special offer price less normal trade terms.

LL0398

(Offer not applicable outside the UK and Republic of Ireland.)

TO BE COMPLETED BY THE CUSTOMER

Name ....

Address ....

....

....

Postcode ....

TO BE COMPLETED BY THE BOOKSELLER

Name ....

Address ....

....

Postcode ....

Account No. ....

Completed vouchers should be sent to: BRF, Livewires Voucher Scheme, Peter's Way, Sandy Lane West, OXFORD, OX4 5HG

TO BE COMPLETED BY THE CUSTOMER

Name ....

Address ....

....

....

Postcode ....

TO BE COMPLETED BY THE BOOKSELLER

Name ....

Address ....

....

Postcode ....

Account No. ....

Completed vouchers should be sent to: BRF, Livewires Voucher Scheme, Peter's Way, Sandy Lane West, OXFORD, OX4 5HG

TO BE COMPLETED BY THE CUSTOMER

Name ....

Address ....

....

....

Postcode ....

TO BE COMPLETED BY THE BOOKSELLER

Name ....

Address ....

....

Postcode ....

Account No. ....

Completed vouchers should be sent to: BRF, Livewires Voucher Scheme, Peter's Way, Sandy Lane West, OXFORD, OX4 5HG

TO BE COMPLETED BY THE CUSTOMER

Name ....

Address ....

....

....

Postcode ....

TO BE COMPLETED BY THE BOOKSELLER

Name ....

Address ....

....

Postcode ....

Account No. ....

Completed vouchers should be sent to: BRF, Livewires Voucher Scheme, Peter's Way, Sandy Lane West, OXFORD, OX4 5HG

TO BE COMPLETED BY THE CUSTOMER

Name ....

Address ....

....

....

Postcode ....

TO BE COMPLETED BY THE BOOKSELLER

Name ....

Address ....

....

Postcode ....

Account No. ....

Completed vouchers should be sent to: BRF, Livewires Voucher Scheme, Peter's Way, Sandy Lane West, OXFORD, OX4 5HG

TO BE COMPLETED BY THE CUSTOMER

Name ....

Address ....

....

....

Postcode ....

TO BE COMPLETED BY THE BOOKSELLER

Name ....

Address ....

....

Postcode ....

Account No. ....

Completed vouchers should be sent to: BRF, Livewires Voucher Scheme, Peter's Way, Sandy Lane West, OXFORD, OX4 5HG

TO BE COMPLETED BY THE CUSTOMER

Name ....

Address ....

....

....

Postcode ....

TO BE COMPLETED BY THE BOOKSELLER

Name ....

Address ....

....

Postcode ....

Account No. ....

Completed vouchers should be sent to: BRF, Livewires Voucher Scheme, Peter's Way, Sandy Lane West, OXFORD, OX4 5HG

TO BE COMPLETED BY THE CUSTOMER

Name ....

Address ....

....

....

Postcode ....

TO BE COMPLETED BY THE BOOKSELLER

Name ....

Address ....

....

Postcode ....

Account No. ....

Completed vouchers should be sent to: BRF, Livewires Voucher Scheme, Peter's Way, Sandy Lane West, OXFORD, OX4 5HG